D0848783

The Joy *of* Mindful Writing

The Joy *of* Mindful Writing

Notes to Inspire Creative Awareness

Joy Kenward

Leaping Hare Press

First published in the UK in 2017 by

Leaping Hare Press

An imprint of The Quarto Group
The Old Brewery, 6 Blundell Street
London N7 9BH, United Kingdom
T (0)20 7700 6700 F (0)20 7700 8066
www.QuartoKnows.com

British Library Cataloguing-in-Publication Data
A catalogue record for this book is available from the British Library

ISBN: 978-1-78240-504-7

This book was conceived, designed and produced by

Leaping Hare Press

58 West Street, Brighton BN1 2RA, United Kingdom
Publisher SUSAN KELLY
Creative Director MICHAEL WHITEHEAD
Editorial Director TOM KITCH
Art Director JAMES LAWRENCE
Commissioning Editor MONICA PERDONI
Project Editor STEPHANIE EVANS
Designer GINNY ZEAL
Illustrator TAKAYO AKIYAMA

Printed in China

10 9 8 7 6 5 4 3 2 1

Contents

INTRODUCTION

When we write, we are speaking – silently and yet with potential power. The writer, sitting alone at a desk, has the universe at the tip of her pen. Through writing, we can transport ourselves and others to the very stars. Using mindfulness in writing provides the opportunity of accessing a deep well of creative awareness. Our whole lives can benefit from this as we begin to experience the joy of written expression through our own creative voice.

MINDFULNESS, THE GENTLE TEACHER

For a child, the business of learning to read and write can feel like a chore. Depending on the teacher, those early classes can make the difference between being able to write fluidly and with confidence or keeping our creative voice muffled inside our heads.

WHEN I WAS TEN YEARS OLD, my class teacher, Mr Lewis, signed my little autograph album, adding the words, 'When you write that book, send me a copy!' This came as a real surprise to me, because I had problems with dyslexia. Although this meant I was a late reader, by the time I was in his class I was reading with enthusiasm. However, writing and spelling were difficult for me. But Mr Lewis was a gifted teacher. He had seen through the poor spelling and messy handwriting, and he had the grace to encourage an imaginative child who loved stories and poetry. The autograph album must have been discarded years ago, but I still have the page with Mr Lewis's autograph – blue ballpoint on yellow paper. It's one of my treasured possessions.

I Dream of Becoming a Writer

After this early encouragement, I decided that I would become a writer. I began stories in my head, jotted down bits of poems, started 'novels'. But most of my creative ideas stayed in my head; they never quite got onto the page. Over the years, I began to overcome the dyslexia that had marred my early attempts at written expression. It wasn't easy; I never could spell naturally. Every word had to be learned individually. But I was lucky with my parents, who helped me patiently with my reading and writing. They encouraged me calmly to concentrate on the sound and shape of each word, to hold a pencil comfortably, to express myself with confidence even if I was unsure of correct spellings. Without knowing it then, I was to recognize this gentle approach many years later as I became aware of mindfulness.

When I left school, someone advised me to learn to type. 'With typing skills you'll always be able to obtain work,' she said. I had ideas of a more creative career, but I lacked confidence, and so I took her advice. It was to prove invaluable to me. Working in an office might not seem the ideal grounding for a creative writer, but it meant I had to write every day. In time, my spelling improved and I began to express myself with ease in my writing – even if it was only politely requesting a customer to pay the bill. And – gift of gifts for a writer – I became a fast and accurate typist. Now that I had the skills and a head full of ideas, what was preventing me from writing it all out in my true creative voice? I still dreamed of being a writer at some time in the future. But in reality, it just wasn't happening.

I had ideas of a more creative career, but I lacked confidence

Writing in the Present Moment

It occurred to me only recently that I didn't start writing until just about the same time that I began to meditate. This was after half a lifetime of talking about being a writer. I still carried my childhood hopes that I would write; I believed I could; I thought about it a lot. But somehow it never quite materialized.

One benefit of meditation is that it provides a sense of present-moment awareness. Meditation helped me to be more interested in 'now' than in the future. Therefore, it became natural for me to carry out what I hoped and believed I could do. And so I began to write and, soon afterwards, to teach creative writing, both of which continue to be a source of great pleasure for me.

Whereas meditation is a highly beneficial pause in life, as valuable to our minds as sleep is to our bodies, mindfulness brings a kind of meditation into our active lives.

Living with Awareness

Mindfulness is about living in a very conscious way. Through mindfulness, we approach our lives and activities with true awareness. This helps us to concentrate deeply upon whatever we wish to focus our attention, and gives us the skills to overcome distractions. For writers, mindfulness allows us to give full attention to our writing, without being distracted by self-judgement, or what I think of as 'the self-doubter'.

'The self-doubter' tells us we are wasting our time; that our writing has no value; that we would be better occupied cleaning the windows; that we might as well be watching TV; that just one more game of solitaire won't make any difference. Such thoughts dwell on lack of confidence, negativity and despondency, rather than giving precedence to the task in hand – the art of writing – which is a valuable task, deserving of our full attention.

A Book for All

This book is by no means only for beginners; I hope it will be of interest to authors and poets who willingly seek new ways of developing their writing, as well as to others who would like to express their thoughts in writing more easily. It is an invitation to work alongside me, perhaps trying for yourself some of the activities I will suggest at various points in the book. When speaking of writers throughout the book, I have opted to use the feminine (for no other reason than that I am female) but, of course, the points I am making address all writers equally.

This is a practical book, giving at least equal consideration to meditative techniques as to writing exercises. This is because I believe that whether we want our writing to be commercially successful, or to allow us to communicate more clearly, or simply to clarify our thoughts and beliefs, writing mindfully can enhance our lives.

CHAPTER ONE

A Mindful Approach

The act of writing is full of space. There is the marvellous space of an empty page, pregnant with possibilities, and the physical space we create between sections or paragraphs. The imaginative space that exists in the action of a story, poem or play can take us to new worlds. And sometimes there's a rather long space when we can't think of what to write next. If we take time to contemplate such spaces quietly, without judgement or fear, they will not seem overwhelming, and we can feel peaceful and adventurous at the same time.

Waiting to Write

The space of non-writing time can be full of promise – a pause before active creativity. For me, this waiting space is an opportunity for meditation, when I can calmly and mindfully contemplate the time-space in which I find myself. I call this 'waiting to write'.

Mindfulness is about living in a very conscious way. For a writer about to begin a piece of work, this means fully attending to the present moment, including the release of any pride or regrets attached to our previous efforts that might have succeeded or not been well received. It also includes detaching ourselves from anxieties and ambitions about the future. Through mindfulness, we approach our lives and activities with present-moment awareness and without judgement, concentrating deeply on the task in hand. This a joyful way of being for anyone. And it is a wonderful advantage for a writer. But it is not always easy.

I personally came to understand mindfulness through meditation. A friend suggested meditation when I was feeling anxious. I agreed to try it, but actually, I was puzzled. 'What is meditation?', I thought. Soon after, I went into my local bookshop and found a little book called *What is Meditation*? I knew that was the one for me. The book is by Osho, a mystic with Buddhist and Hindu roots. That book taught me, in very simple terms, the basics of mindfulness meditation.

Beginning with five minutes every day, it soon felt easy and natural to increase the time I spent meditating. Now it's an important part of my life. When I'm meditating regularly, everything runs more smoothly, I feel less anxious, more serene and (magically) I seem to have a lot more time.

Time to Write

Many people intend to write. But without mindfulness, this intention will often remain just that – an intention – and is never actually carried out. Nearly every student joining my Beginners' classes tells me that they've been meaning to write for a long time. They've had ideas but never quite started; or they've started but the whole thing fizzled out. The reasons are various, but they are generally on a theme of time – being too busy, procrastination, not having enough hours in the day. For whatever reason, time seems to be the problem.

TRY IT NOW

As you are now, with this book in your hand, bring your attention to your own breathing. Take a few slow, gentle breaths, noticing the air flowing through your nostrils or your mouth. Feel the differences in temperature as it passes in and out of your body. While you breathe, be aware of the weight and texture of this book. For these moments, it's just you, your breath and the book, with no other thoughts to disturb you. That is peace. That is mindfulness.

But is this true? It can be easy to blame lack of time when what we really lack is confidence. It is very often self-doubt that actually stops us writing. If we are able to accept that we feel self-doubt, we might also accept that there are ways to find time to write.

The Self-Doubt Block

Even for experienced writers, an idea that began well might suddenly and unaccountably become obstructed; out of the blue they feel 'blocked'. Perhaps they've begun a story, but find it difficult to proceed; they know what they want to say, but can't quite express it in the fullest way. The creative flow dries up or begins to run off course. They've lost confidence.

Writing is an extension of thinking. At its best it flows, dances, marches or twirls to the pace of our most conscious and creative imagination. Alone in our heads, at our desk, composing and writing freely, this can be easy, peaceful and beautiful. But it is when we actually have to express our thoughts to others that we often encounter difficulty. That's when we become uncertain about using the appropriate words and the correct spelling and grammar; about impressing, helping or affecting others. Self-doubt enters the writing space and fills our minds with negative thoughts.

Moving on in life always includes acceptance

Controlling the Mind

Because writing is so very close to thinking, we need to be able to see beyond any negative thoughts and get closer to the joyful heart of our own creativity. This is where practising mindfulness meditation can help. Before we write, we need to have a practical and positive relationship with our mind, one in which we accept feelings such as self-doubt, but remain in control. This is not a strict kind of control, but a peaceful freedom that recognizes problems and yet resolutely concentrates on our central intention, which is to write.

Moving on in life always includes acceptance. When I began to teach, I worried about my dyslexia. How could I set myself up as a teacher of creative writing when I often forgot how to spell a word, especially when writing on a large whiteboard in front of a class? Mindfulness helped me to accept this problem and to see beyond it to my central intention, which was to help and inspire students with their creative writing.

At the beginning of a course, I would tell the students about my dyslexia and explain to them that I sometimes needed help with spelling, inviting anyone to speak up if they noticed it. They became used to occasionally calling out spelling suggestions when I was stuck. Together we would discuss the construction and sound of words, and explore the wealth of dictionaries and other reference data available to us. Those classes became a collaboration of learning, where no one judged each other's perceived limitations. In fact, my dyslexia

MINDFULNESS EXERCISE

A 'WAITING TO WRITE' MEDITATION

Next time you feel 'blocked' as a writer, try this simple exercise:

- Sit quietly, relaxed, but with your back as upright as possible, supported with cushions, if necessary.
- Close your eyes.
- Notice your breathing. As the air enters your nostrils, it will feel a little cool; as it exhales, it will feel a little warmer. Try to notice this without comment or judgement.
- Thoughts will come into your mind – for example, 'What does any of this have to do with my writer's block?'
- Notice the thought. Accept it without judgement.
- Notice the emotion that comes with the thought. How does it feel? Give your attention to the feeling without naming or judging it.
- Now bring your attention back to your breath.
- Every time a thought comes into your mind, accept the thought, notice how it feels without judgement, and bring your attention back to the breath.

With perseverance, ten minutes of this meditation every day will help; half an hour would be much better. At the least, it will help you to feel relaxed and more in control of your mind and emotions. At best, you will soon be writing freely, without anxiety.

became a blessing, because any students who had similar problems saw me as someone who had overcome this long-standing difficulty to the extent of writing a number of novels and qualifying as a teacher. This helped to give them belief in their ability and confidence to rise above problems of their own.

Materials

All our creative ideas begin in the mind, but writing itself starts with the action of making marks on a page. Choosing the right writing materials can make the difference between writing effortlessly or feeling cramped and uncomfortable – which, of course, affects the ease with which our writing flows.

Many writers hope that their finished writing will be in the form of a printed work. Ideally, this would be a book that has been edited and designed by a publisher, and produced in large numbers (hopefully) by a professional printer. We may spend some time imagining our beautifully illustrated, skilfully created, prize-winning novel taking up room on bookshop shelves and bedside tables all over the world. We spend less time considering the importance of the original materials of writing – our own pens, notebooks, laptops and similar – which are actually essential to the creation of our writing and the ease with which it flows.

In the same way, we often worry about our appearance – our clothes, hairstyle, shoes and other superficialities. And yet, when we take time to really consider, we know that the workings of our bodies, the health of our internal organs, the protection afforded by our skin, are significantly more important than our physical appearance. They are, of course, absolutely essential to our very lives. In meditation, we often concentrate on our breath because it is the one vital action of our bodies that we can easily be aware of. Without our breath, we could literally do nothing.

Mindfulness teaches us to notice what is fundamental to our being; to notice and to gently give time and respect to it. And mindfulness can also teach us to value the tools of our writing trade: to choose them with care, and to afford them the attention and respect that they deserve. As our breath supports and allows our very life, so our pens and paper give substance to our creative writing efforts. We can't expect to always be thinking about our breath or our writing materials, but we can decide to give them regular mindful attention, especially when we are beginning a writing session.

Beginning Again

Whether you are an experienced writer, beginner or anything in between, I would like to suggest that you allow yourself now to 'begin again' with your writing materials, choosing them mindfully, watchfully, with respect and concentration.

What materials do you use for writing? Personally, I often compose my work directly on my laptop. However, when I'm beginning a new piece of work or a new section, I nearly always handwrite it and then copy it onto my laptop later. Handwriting necessitates real, physical movement and a more sensual experience – the texture of the paper, the press of the pen as the stream (or trickle) of words emerges from it. This is an almost magical action – as thoughts become converted into words and exist in a physical way. This is a new creation!

Thoughts on Crossing-Out

Some people prefer to use a pencil so that they can easily erase words or phrases. However, I wouldn't advise using an eraser. As this handwriting is just a draft, crossing-out doesn't matter, and you might sometimes want to go back to your original thoughts and words. They should be easy to see under the crossing-out. If they've been erased, they are lost. The same problem can occur with using word-processing software. Of course, it is possible to keep every version, but this can in itself be time-consuming and a writer could 'lose the flow' while negotiating the machinations of software. For me, although I'm happy usually to write directly onto my laptop, it's different when I'm composing a poem. For poetry, I nearly always use a pen or pencil on paper. The essayist and poet Paul Valéry apparently said, 'A poem is never finished, only abandoned.' Certainly, I keep coming back to my poems time and again,

making alterations, but I often decide that I prefer an earlier version. That's when I'm glad I still have the first jottings of the poem in my notebook. Despite the crossings-out and reworkings, I can usually decipher the original version. Although I do eventually type and print them out, my file of printed poems is still decorated with corrections and crossings-out.

MINDFULNESS EXERCISE

CHOOSING WITH AWARENESS

Mindfully, giving full attention to your task, bring together some new writing materials (they needn't be new purchases; you can choose from items you already have).

- Choose a pen. How does it feel in your hand? Is it comfortable? Does the ink flow freely? Some people prefer to use a fountain pen, because the free-flow of the ink can be much more effortless than using a ballpoint pen, which has to be pressed onto the paper in order for the ink to appear – sometimes causing painful 'writer's cramp' in the hand. Or perhaps you would rather use a pencil. Is it the right length and weight? Does it need sharpening?
- Now, choose some paper. What do you prefer? An A4 or A5 notebook? Hardback or soft? Lined or unlined? Choose just the kind of notebook that feels right to you – or no notebook at all; you can write on single sheets of white or coloured paper if you wish. When you're selecting paper, or a notebook, choose mindfully. Touch the surface of the paper with the flat of your hand. How does it feel? Be aware of its texture.

The Power of the Pen

Some highly successful authors use simple materials for writing: a favourite pen and particular type of notebook for example, or an ancient typewriter. This might be thought of as rather idiosyncratic, but a great writer is entitled to have idiosyncrasies, and so are you!

If, like me, you normally use a computer or laptop, I would like to suggest, just for the sake of the exercise on the facing page, that you try using a pen or pencil and paper for a short time. To me, there is something both active and powerful about the hand movement as thoughts are written down with a pen. The pen seems almost like an extension of the hand, and so the thoughts come – physically and directly – from the mind onto the page.

Place and Time

As writers, we all need a place to write and the opportunity to do so. How important is a particular time and place to a writer? Each of us is different, but if we keep a clear mind, uncluttered by preconceptions, we can find unexpected opportunities for writing time.

What time of day do you feel most creative? Scientific studies show people perform cognitive and imaginative tasks better in the mornings. Other studies cast doubt on this. I think it is probably different for every writer,

but it's worth experimenting mindfully. To be mindful means to be fully present, fully 'awake' to the reality of our lives. So, ask yourself, what is the most convenient time for you to write? Early morning? Late at night? In your lunch break? On a train journey to work? Once you try, you might find that a convenient time also feels like a good time for you. Experiment and be adventurous. Allow yourself the time to write.

If it feels right, aim to find a place that's fairly quiet and likely to be free from interruptions. Try to ensure that other people respect the time you need to do your writing. Don't let them distract you; and don't be distracted either by 'the self-doubter' telling you to clean the car, weed the garden, or do any other chore that distracts you from creative work. Don't worry: once your pen is on the paper, the 'self-doubter' in your head does tend to fade.

Making Time

You may feel that you have little choice with regard to time and place for writing, especially if your life is circumscribed by work and family commitments. You could try going to bed an hour later than normal and spending that hour writing. Or you could set your alarm an hour earlier than usual and write for an hour before your normal day begins. I did this myself when I still had a full-time job with office hours. After the initial physical resistance, I enjoyed being awake and working at my writing in the very early mornings.

Someone once told me that she gave up one TV programme per evening and spent the time writing. Within six months she had written a novel. So, if you feel short of time, consider whether something you do regularly could be put aside and spend the time writing instead. If this seems impossible, try to sit with the impossibility for a while. Consider it mindfully. Often, choices appear where we least expect them.

Go Out to Write

If you feel there is no chance that you will be able to concentrate at home, try going out to do your writing. Public libraries have quiet areas where there are desks and chairs. J.K. Rowling apparently wrote a lot of *Harry Potter* in a café, with people around her. Why not try the same? This certainly would prevent the distractions of chores and other responsibilities at home. I often write in a café in my home town. It is spacious and quiet, with comfortable chairs. I always buy at least one drink, and I've never been asked to leave!

Don't be constrained by negative assumptions, and don't be constrained by convention. Virginia Woolf's idea of having 'A Room of One's Own' was just right for her. What you are watching for is – what is right for you? What is right for us might not be our dream soundproof room with the best of writing materials, computer technology and a lovely view. However, if we plan with awareness, 'what's right for us' will be the best we can do in our present circumstances.

Buy a small notebook and carry it with you all the time, making 'snapshots' in words rather than pictures of anything that takes your interest (scraps of conversation, quirks of nature, odd personalities, striking sights and sounds). With this, you can write wherever and whenever you have the opportunity. Use the notebook as a sourcebook for your writing. It's also very useful for recording any brilliant ideas that otherwise would be forgotten by the time you get home.

If we approach problems mindfully, the problems disappear and we are left with opportunities, and the choice of whether or not to use them.

The Scent of Confidence

Sense of smell is very evocative. Certain scents restore emotions and feelings so that we relive them in the present moment. If we choose and especially if we practise, we can produce a similar effect through mindfulness, reviving helpful emotions to assist with our creative writing.

Are there certain scents that bring back memories to you? For me, the scent of lavender always carries me back and puts me in the body of my six-year-old self, sitting in my grandmother's kitchen, filling lavender bags. It isn't just the memory, it's the feeling of safety, of love all around me, and of being absorbed in an interesting activity.

Here is another question for you: What inspires you? Especially, what increases your faith in your own ability to write? Sit quietly and relaxed, and think back. Is there a piece of writing you have done that particularly pleases you? You might have had praise from a friend or success in a writing competition. There may be a book or poem you have read that filled you with enthusiasm and inspiration. Perhaps something happened in

MINDFULNESS EXERCISE

CONFIDENCE SCENT MEDITATION

Sit quietly, as before, relaxed, but with your back as upright as possible, supported by cushions, if necessary.

- Close your eyes.
- Notice your breathing. As the air enters your nostrils, it will feel a little cool; as it exhales, it will feel a little warmer. Try to notice this without comment or judgement.
- As you relax into the rhythm of breathing, bring your 'confidence scent' to mind. Recall the memory that caused this positive emotion. Notice the emotion and how it feels. Try to detach it from the circumstances that brought it about. Now it is a simple, pleasurable, uplifting emotion, unattached to any thought or memory.
- Imagine gently inhaling this 'confidence scent' with your breath.
- Every in-breath brings refreshment and inspiration.
- Every out-breath brings warmth and confidence.

Return to this simple 'confidence scent' meditation whenever you feel the need for some extra self-belief, especially before writing.

your life to boost your self-belief. It doesn't matter how long ago or in what circumstances this happened. The important thing is that it increases your enthusiasm and confidence.

A Warm Memory

Personally, a memory comes to mind from more than twenty years ago: I am at college, studying English Literature at evening classes. I'm in the lift, going up to the classroom on the fifth floor, and my tutor, Mr Darke, is also in the lift. He is turning to me and saying, 'Joy, your Hamlet essay was good. It was good.' The feeling I received from this praise is warm, uplifting, confident, supporting. Over the years, I've received other praise, some success and personal satisfaction for my writing. And yet, after all this time, it's still that memory of praise from my tutor that I turn to when I want to give myself confidence. I call the emotion that comes from that memory my 'confidence scent', because it returns me to that uplifting, positive feeling as powerfully as the scent of lavender returns me to my grandmother's kitchen.

So, I ask again: what raises your faith in your own ability? How does it make you feel? Notice this thought or memory without judgement. Notice the emotion that comes with it. How does that feel? Try to give your attention to the feeling without attaching it to the original thought or memory. Try not to name or judge it. Try to experience it like a scent that you can inhale with your breath.

Beginning

So, what next? With mindfulness practice, the writer sits in a space of creative awareness. At any point she can relax into mindfulness and summon her 'confidence scent'. It is the right time and place. On the table she has her chosen writing materials. It's time to begin.

Now (at last!) let's do some writing. There is only one way to begin to write: that is just to do it. I think you knew that already.

When students join my classes, I always advise them to write every day. There are various types of daily writing to choose from. Some people write in a journal, recording daily activities. 'Morning Pages' are similar, but written for a set period of time or a set number of pages. When I wrote 'Morning Pages', I tried to write without stopping for half an hour. Sometimes the result was a rather banal set of pages. Other times, I was surprised by the lucidity of my writing. In 'Morning Pages' people often write about their own lives, feelings, activities, people they meet, their reactions, emotions, conversations. It is a 'meandering' kind of writing that can be useful and liberating. If nothing else, the regular practice of expressing ourselves in words must be good for our writing.

But, for the purpose of this gentle, mindful approach to writing, I'd like you to begin with a very simple exercise, even if you are an experienced writer. First I will ask you to

choose from a few words; next, before you begin, I'll suggest a short meditation; then, for ten minutes, I'd like you to do a piece of writing based on the following.

Stream of Consciousness Writing

This is another regular method of writing, which I always introduce early on in my creative writing courses. We do this for ten minutes at the beginning of every class. Stream of consciousness writing is sometimes also called 'internal monologue' and is a literary style employed most famously by James Joyce, in his novel *Ulysses*. Other authors, including Virginia Woolf, also used this style. It is characterized by thoughts, feelings and reactions, and is not generally expected to include objective description or dialogue. This makes it an ideal method for daily writing.

I think of stream of consciousness writing as being a mindful process. The way it works is that we choose a subject or a word at random and, beginning with that, let ourselves go, writing whatever comes to mind for just ten minutes (or longer, if we have time). As in meditation, we are watching the mind, but now we are also writing down what we see. For example, if the subject or set word was 'stone', I might start writing about the pebbles on a beach I know in Devon, and go on to describe the sea there in all its moods. This might turn my thoughts to ships and the distant countries to which they sail – so that I could finish by

writing about the similarities and differences between the different peoples of the world, and speculating on the origins of the human race.

Go Where Your Mind Takes You

Of course, such meanderings will not always happen – not in ten minutes anyway. Instead, such an exercise could result in a piece of writing that is intensely descriptive of a single object – or maybe a series of unconnected notes. The idea is just to go wherever your mind takes you. Perhaps you might already be used to writing in this way, or you may never have tried it before. Ideally, this is something that would benefit writers to do every day, along with meditation. It's rather like a pianist practising scales or a mechanic maintaining an engine. Ten minutes isn't very long to set aside each day in order to keep our 'writerly' cogs oiled.

If you can't think of a subject for your writing, pick a word at random from a dictionary, or just look around you for something to start you off. Go wherever your mind takes you.

I believe it is important that you keep this daily writing to yourself. My reason for this is that it's good to write completely without reserve, without worrying whether you will or will not provoke a reader's annoyance, approval, pleasure or judgement. We usually do consider our reader; that's important. But for ten minutes per day, we should be free to write without such concerns, enabling us to try different

MINDFULNESS EXERCISE

THE STREAM OF CONSCIOUSNESS MEDITATION

This mindful activity is a beneficial one for any writer, whether they are using the latest speech-recognition technology or a pencil and paper; whether they are writing the latest in a series of successful TV dramas or a letter to a friend. When you are a successful author, remember it!

- Gather your chosen writing materials and sit comfortably, ready to write, with them in front of you.
- Please select one of the following words and write it at the top of your page:

  Hand Wave Box Hill Ice

- Turn your attention to your breath. As before, notice how the air feels a little cool as it enters your nostrils; a little warmer as you exhale. Concentrate on your breath for a few minutes, then, as you breathe, call up the feeling of your 'confidence scent' and allow it to be inhaled along with the air. When other thoughts enter your mind, notice them without judgement and gently bring your attention back to your breath and your 'confidence scent'.
- Now, bring your attention to your writing materials. Notice their shape and texture. Contemplate them while maintaining the rhythm of your breath and the feeling of your 'confidence scent'. After a few minutes, pick up your pen or pencil and begin the stream of consciousness exercise, beginning with the word you have chosen and following wherever your mind takes you.

styles and subjects, and express opinions or emotions as the 'stream' dictates. So, stream of consciousness writing is for your eyes only. Keep it private. If you wish, you may use it in the future as material for stories, poetry or anything you like.

Writing Mindfully

I aim to use mindfulness with my writing. So when, for example, I'm beginning a new chapter of my novel, I try to form a strong awareness of my intention for the characters, situation and plot. Then I prepare my materials (pen, pencil, paper and laptop) and, sitting as comfortably as I can, quietly discard from my mind all other worries or considerations. This is my 'waiting' time. As I inhale and exhale, I introduce to my mind the feeling of my 'confidence scent'. Other thoughts will inevitably enter my mind, but I gently return to the contemplation of my writing materials. In the back of my mind are ideas for my new chapter; I may have already made some notes, but for the time being I am just 'waiting'. After a certain period of time, when my mind feels settled and not too many thoughts are coming in to disturb the stillness, I allow the new chapter ideas to come to the fore. I pick up my pen or activate my laptop, and begin to write.

I try to form a strong awareness of my intention

CHAPTER TWO

WRITING WITH AWARENESS

If, as writers, we approach our own lives with conscious awareness, then we can hope to convey feelings, experiences and emotions realistically in our writing. Regularly practising mindfulness meditation generates potent awareness in our minds. And this has another beautiful effect – it provides the true happiness that comes with a peaceful mind. Every experience, whether emotional, physical or spiritual, can be viewed through a peaceful mind. Far from weakening the intensity of experience, this actually enables us to know it with deeper clarity, so that our writing can convincingly reflect reality.

The Senses

We know the world we live in through our five physical senses: sight, hearing, touch, taste, smell. They are our direct line to the universe. By referring to the physical senses, we can allow the reader to enter and understand the world we are creating with our writing.

How do you feel at this moment? Is your body relaxed? Do you experience a pain somewhere? Are you hot or cold? Is there any discomfort you hadn't noticed before? Bringing awareness to our lives, and particularly to the act of writing, provides the hope of depicting with clarity our own experiences and those of any fictional world we are creating. Consider, for example, that you might very well be able to describe an experience of working in your own garden. But how does that actually feel to be gardening? Can you recreate this in words to the extent that your reader pictures her own hands plunged into the soil and feels its texture in her imagination?

Writing does not always have to evoke this depth of sensual experience, but practising written description using the

By referring to the physical senses we can allow the reader to enter and understand the world we are creating with our writing

senses can very much improve the quality and expression of our writing. The best way to begin this is through mindfulness – and it is huge fun!

Engaging the Senses

Living mindfully very much includes the senses. Put your hand flat on the page now. Feel the temperature of the page. Curl your fingers slightly and feel the texture of the paper's surface. There is no judgement in this exercise, it is simple awareness. Try it again with your hand against another surface – a table, a piece of clothing you are wearing, your own hair or skin.

There is nothing quite like the texture of a peach

Now, let's taste something – oh, let it be a peach, because it's summer now as I am writing, and peaches happen to be in season (and I love them). There is nothing quite like the texture of a peach, is there? What is that like against your lips? And when you bite into it? What happens with the juice?

Listen. There might be music playing as you read this. But don't be distracted by the music. Listen. What else can you hear? It might be traffic in the street nearby, but don't name it 'traffic'; just be aware of its pure sound. Listen for the little thumps and clicks of life going on around you. Don't name or judge them, just give them your attention.

Close your eyes for a moment. What did you see? Nothing? Try again and move your head from side to side this time. If there is sunshine, trees and a breeze, you might be aware of red flashes against your closed eyes; a pale grey near the light; a deeper grey where there are shadows.

Raise the book to your nose. Does it have a scent? Do the same with the palm of your hand. We don't have much language for scents. We have to use metaphors. Have you ever listened to wine experts sniffing and tasting and describing wines? 'Summer garden.' 'Wood notes.' 'A compost heap.' They use metaphors because of the dearth of words for describing scents. But this lack of language actually helps us to smell mindfully. Get close to that banana skin, or that pot of pencils. Just experience the smell.

A Secret Key to Memory and Imagination

Real life is a wonderful source of drama and emotion, which we can use for our writing. Everyone has at least one story to tell about their lives: 'Walking to Everest Base Camp', 'Giving birth for the first time', 'Meeting the love of my life'. It's the same when we think of interesting people. Most of us know a remarkable individual or two who have performed exploits, displayed eccentric behaviour, or achieved accomplishments that are far beyond ordinary. (In fact, there can be difficulties in using real people and their experiences for our fiction writing, and both are best disguised as much as possible.) Such real stories and

MINDFULNESS EXERCISE

A SENSES WRITING EXERCISE

- Bring your writing materials together. As described on pages 37–8, be aware of the messages you are receiving from your senses. Sit comfortably and take some slow breaths, noticing the temperature of the air as it enters and leaves your body. Although you have been thinking earlier about the senses, and how awareness of them can help your writing, for the time being, you are concentrating only on your breathing; you are 'waiting to write'.
- Now, choose some paper and a pen. I would like you to write a page about each of your senses.
- Beginning with the sense of sight, start to write what you can see. If there is a particular colour in front of your eyes, let that colour lead you to some other place. A yellow duster, for instance, might take you to a beach and provide a memory of a distant time, or an imaginary scene. How many words are there that mean 'yellow'? How many different shades and names are there for that one colour? Make friends with those words – ochre, amber, brimstone, buttercup and all the others. Write them and then read them aloud. How beautiful! Let your mind and your writing take you on a mystery tour but, from time to time, bring your attention back to the sense of sight. What else can you see? Where does it lead you?
- When you have filled one page, begin again with another of your senses, and then again until you have filled five pages. You are writing for yourself. Be adventurous. You may create fresh ways of presenting an experience in words. If you think a slice of apple 'sparkles' on the tongue, then 'sparkle' can become a true word for the taste of apple.

personalities usually sit at the top of our minds, ready to come out when we're talking with friends, and readily accessible in writing sessions. But we all have another source of inspiration that is not usually reached so easily.

Deep within our subconscious are memories that can provide treasure for our writing. The imagination itself is a magical thing, putting together fragments of knowledge and memory to create wonderful, original characters, situations and modes of expression. And there is a secret key that can open the door to these subconscious imagination-feeders, and it is remarkably simple: make a list.

The List-Making Technique

I always bring this list-making technique to my classes, and although my students often begin by being sceptical, nearly everyone finds that it awakens memories they had thought lost, or brings an unexpected slant to an old idea. The important thing with this exercise is to write quickly. In the same way that mindfulness meditation requires us to have present-moment awareness without judgement, so list-making for creative writing needs us to remember without analysis. Don't think too much; just write.

nearly everyone finds it awakens memories they had thought lost

To begin with, I invite you to try the list-writing exercise on the facing page. For this, you'll be writing a list of all the

MINDFULNESS EXERCISE

A LIST-WRITING AND SENSES MEDITATION

- Begin by once more gathering together your writing materials and ensuring you are comfortable. As before, take a few deep breaths, noticing without judgement the temperature of the air as you inhale and exhale.
- The task is to write a list of all the places you can remember being in your life, from the mundane, like a dentist's waiting room, to the sublime, like a mountain path. Don't judge these as being 'interesting', 'important' or 'dull'. Just relax and write as quickly as you can. Don't enlarge on the memory for the time being, just make a simple list, as long as possible, for about five minutes.

Keep this list – it might be useful later when you are out of ideas.

- Next, look back at your list and choose just one of those places as your subject. Imagine yourself back in that place, standing, sitting or lying there. What can you touch, see, taste, smell and hear? Consider each of the senses. Does any one of them take precedence in this place? Are they all equally essential to your experience of this memory? Make rough notes for ten to fifteen minutes.
- Now try writing up your notes into a page or two, using full sentences this time and enlarging on your memory. You can write it as if it's an entry in your diary or a letter to a friend, a piece in a magazine, or even a scene in a fictional story. At this stage, you might decide to leave out some of your 'senses' notes, depending on whether or not they fit into the mood of your written piece. The senses help to make a written description real to the reader. However, like spice in a cake, this 'literary flavouring' needs to be used sparingly. It should serve your writing, not overwhelm it.

places you can remember being in your life, from somewhere you went on holiday as a child to the bus stop where you were standing this morning. Don't start yet. First let's think about what constitutes a 'place'. In our classes, we decided that a 'place' is somewhere that we can actually *be*, in a physical sense; so the smallest 'place' could be, say, a cupboard, and the biggest the planet Earth (although others suggested 'the womb' and 'the universe'). 'Places' also include towns, countries, gardens, vehicles, aircraft, and several others. For this exercise, it's important to write everything we can think of, including (and probably especially) places that don't seem interesting or important.

The Senses in Fiction Writing

We cannot do better for our fictional characters than to put ourselves in their place, just as, in the exercise here, we stepped back into a memory of a place we have been before. If your fictional character is, for example, walking on a beach, imagine the sand between their toes. Depending on the personality of the character, would this be a pleasurable sensation or irritating? Perhaps they don't notice it at all, because they are overwhelmed by the aroma and taste of a delicious piece of fruit or ice cream they are eating as they walk. In turn, this may cause them not to notice something important in the story – the signs of a crime scene or the significant glance of a stranger.

MINDFULNESS EXERCISE

USING OBJECTS FOR CHARACTERIZATION

- First, gather together some objects to represent each of the senses. In my classes, I use a torch for sight, a bell for hearing, a satin ribbon and piece of sandpaper for touch, sweets for taste and lavender for smell, but choose whatever is right for you.
- Have your writing materials with you.
- Create a simple character in your mind – a man or a woman. Jot down a few details about them. Give them a name, an occupation and whether they have a family, a job, a circle of friends. Describe the most important thing in their life. What do they wish for?
- Now imagine him or her in a setting. This could be a building or landscape you know yourself or imaginary ones.
- With the knowledge of this character and setting in your mind, it's time for a few 'waiting to write' minutes. Don't underestimate the value of such a pause before writing. And don't worry that you will forget what you've decided about the character, as you have your notes; so sit quietly and relaxed for a while, turn your attention to the breath, and close your eyes. Notice without judgement any thoughts that come to your mind, but don't cling to them; bring your attention mindfully back to your breathing and the temperature of the air as you inhale and exhale.
- When your thoughts have quietened, give your attention to the objects you chose to represent the senses.
- Bring to mind the character you have created. They are in the setting you've decided upon, going about their business, when one of those objects, with its sensual properties, is dropped into their world. How does this happen and how do they experience the object? Write it all down, remembering the senses.

THE ELEMENTS

The tradition of the elements begins in mythology, and has mystical as well as scientific origins. The four traditional elements are fire, earth, air and water. Almost anything we know can be associated with one of these, and they provide writerly inspiration for stories, poems, memoirs and so on.

EVERY ANCIENT CIVILIZATION, whether or not they had begun to develop scientific investigation, had a concept of the elements. The four main elements were often afforded human names and personalities, and were thought to have powers beyond what could be observed and known in an objective way. This desire to make sense of the physical world was probably what inspired the very first storytellers, even before human beings began to use written language. We still use the elements metaphorically all the time, for example, speaking of people as being 'down to earth', or having a 'fiery personality', perhaps accusing someone of having 'watered-down' principles or being an 'airhead'.

For writers, the elements can provide inspiration to shape and develop their work.

For example, I might describe a summer's day when I was on a beach with friends. We took swimming gear, a picnic and, importantly, one couple joined us, bringing with them their new baby. My primary memory of that day is of us all cooing

over and caring for the baby, passing her around between us. But I pause for a moment, wondering how to express the essence of my memory. Sitting quietly, breathing mindfully, I wait, and then introduce the idea of the elements. I begin with fire – and think of the barbeque someone lit. That reminds me of the other major source of fiery heat that day, the sun – how bright and strong it was, and how the fair-skinned baby was slightly sunburnt, despite the parasol we put over her. We learned that day about the strength of the sun, the thinness of sunshade fabric and the vulnerability of a baby's skin. And my memoir has taken a turn away from simple memory, providing a caution for readers who might spend a day in the sun with a young family.

The Mythological Gods of the Elements

In mythology the four elements are personified as deities.

Fire

The Greek god, Hephaestus, was known as the god of fire and became the protector-deity for blacksmiths and other artisans working with fire. Some sources describe him as having a kind and generous personality, enjoying creating gifts for his friends. Hephaestus was, however, prone to jealousy. In fact, he could be seen as an ideal, multi-faceted character for fiction. Fire can provide action and drama for our writing: an erupting volcano – or a batch of burnt cakes. It can bring

brightness, colour and warmth, fireworks or a comfortable family hearth. And we can use fire in a more abstract way, introducing the facets of fire into a character's personality – brilliance, quickness of movement or smouldering mood.

Earth

The goddess of earth was Demeter, who gave life to the grain, controlled the harvest and was in charge of the fertility of the earth. The ancient Greeks would present the first loaf of the year to Demeter's altar, in thanks for the harvest. For us, it's worth remembering that earth gives texture and presence to our writing, providing the landscape of our settings and helping to make real the world in which our fictional characters exist. With regard to characters, you might think of an 'earthy' character as someone with a steady personality, perhaps reliable and calm. Imagine introducing a metaphorical 'earthquake' into this character's story. What would make an 'earthy' character 'quake' and how would they react?

Air

The god of air (and the sky) was Zeus. He was in charge of the weather and was also the King of the gods, perhaps because, as the air god, he was higher than all the others. Zeus, despite his 'airy' position, had a reputation for fieriness, going about with a lightning bolt as a staff, demanding his own way, and getting into trouble with women. If I were to describe someone as being 'airy', I would tend to present them as rather delicate and dreamy. But thinking of Zeus reminds me that an 'airy' person could have hidden traits, such as dazzling beauty like the summer sky or the ominous menace of gathering thunderclouds.

Water

Poseidon was the god of the oceans and all waters. His hair and beard were blue and he carried a trident with which he could strike the Earth, causing seismic upheaval. Sailors traditionally revered Poseidon, and would beg him to calm storms at sea or provide convenient currents or ocean breezes to speed their voyages. Poseidon reminds us of the power of water. When we consider that without water there could be no life, we can see its power as nurturing as well as potentially destructive. To describe someone's personality as 'watery' really doesn't seem at all positive, but, as writers, we may provide our fictional characters with some of the peaceful or stormy qualities of water, to dramatic effect.

The Elemental Pilgrimage

Although we might find examples of the elements anywhere to inspire our writing, there is nothing like the great outdoors to bring them close to our attention. On Monday mornings, I always travel to the Chalice Well in Glastonbury, which is some miles from where I live. Chalice Well is a World Peace

Garden, with the motto 'Many Paths, One Source', and people of many different faiths make a pilgrimage from all over the world to visit the garden and drink water from the well. I have a voluntary job there on Mondays, serving in the wonderful book and gift shop. Travelling to Glastonbury is a weekly pilgrimage for me. I go there by bus and it's always a long journey, so I leave the house at just after six thirty in the morning. At any season of the year, that's a lovely time of day to be up and about. It takes me about twenty minutes to walk to the bus stop. As I step out of my front door, the first thing I notice is the quality of the air. Whether it is still or breezy, there is always a fineness to the air at that time of day. My footsteps on the pavement are like a walking meditation, as my feet connect with the Earth. In the winter, I often see the first beams of sunlight over the horizon – the fire-god of day rising to bless the Earth. If it's raining, I don't need to seek the element of water, but even at the driest time of year, she is evident in all life: every tree, every garden flower, every person I meet. And the elements are abundant with inspiration for a writer – especially out of doors, especially in the early morning.

The great Buddhist teacher Thich Nhat Hanh advocates walking meditation, which is when we concentrate deeply on the sensation of our feet stepping and moving on the Earth. This idea can be incorporated into a walking meditation for writers, where we are mindfully aware, experiencing all the elements as we walk.

MINDFULNESS EXERCISE

A WALKING 'ELEMENTS' MEDITATION

- If you can, prepare to go out for a walk, either in the countryside, or around the streets near to where you live. If you have a garden, you might prefer to walk in this familiar space. Dress suitably, depending on the weather (I live in England and rarely go out without an umbrella at any time of year!), and, because you are a writer, I trust you will have a pen and notebook in your pocket.
- Before leaving the house, take a pleasant, mindful breath or two, remembering that you are about to embark on a meditative walk.
- As you step out, notice the sensation of the air on your face and body. Walk at a comfortable speed, feeling your feet connect with the Earth, whether through a firm pavement, a grassy lawn or another surface. Be aware of the quality of the light, noticing your physical reaction to this, the brightest of elements. If it rains, you might need an umbrella or raincoat, or you could choose to experience the sensation of the drops on your head, face and body. Even in dry weather, the nurturing power of water will be present, along with the other elements, in the life of people, animals and plants. Try not to evaluate or analyse these realities; just be aware and enjoy the experience of this present walking moment.
- I hope you will return from your walk more fully awake to the four elements in the experience of life.
- And now, it's time for writing. Try to fully express your feelings, positive or negative, about the walk, especially remembering your awareness of the elements. You could write this into a journal entry, fictional story, lyric poem or any other form of writing that you choose.

The Seasons

From my study window in Somerset, England, I look down over a gentle valley towards the undulating landscape of the Mendip Hills. My view is more than half sky, and I see both land and air in every seasonal mood. Continually changing, it provides constant inspiration for my writing.

On a spinning planet, we expect changes all the time, even in countries where there are no discernible seasons. In England where I live, our seasons are defined as winter at the beginning of the year, and summer in the middle, with spring and autumn in between. However, these traditional seasons bring many surprises. We sometimes talk about this with disappointment – and even indignation – as if the seasons should be set in a rigid pattern. Spring is supposed to bring new life after a winter sleep; summer is all growth and warmth; autumn flames colourful and abundant; and winter pictures crisp snow and bright Yule or New Year celebrations. The truth is less defined. I've seen frost in August, daffodils in January, balmy sunny days in December with roses blooming; and bitter cold, rain and storms at any time during the year.

No matter how nature provides constant evidence that seasonal changes rarely fit the pattern we imagine, we continue to create art, literature (and calendar illustrations) that

confirm our expectations. The seasons do pepper literature with some of its most memorable images. Who can forget Dickens's description of a cheerful Ebenezer Scrooge, joyfully opening his casement window on a crisp, cold, sunny Christmas day? Or E. M. Forster's scene of young love in a field of springtime violets (see page 52)?

As those great writers understood, the seasons provide plenty of material for our writing, giving metaphor and mood to our poetry and lending authenticity to the world of fictional characters. A description of a character gathering spring blossom, or tramping through an icy landscape, can give the impression of the passage of time in a story, help shape the narrative, and provide opportunities for originality. Imagine writing the typical scenario of 'boy meets girl' but in four different seasons and four changes of weather. What happens to a romantic scene on a moonlit beach when there's a sudden rainstorm?

Running to the window, he opened it, and
put out his head. No fog, no mist; clear, bright, jovial,
stirring, cold; cold, piping for the blood to dance to;
golden sunlight; heavenly sky; sweet fresh air...

FROM 'A CHRISTMAS CAROL' BY CHARLES DICKENS (1812–70)
ENGLISH NOVELIST AND SOCIAL CAMPAIGNER

For a moment he contemplated her, as one who had fallen out of heaven. He saw radiant joy in her face, he saw the flowers beat against her dress in blue waves. The bushes above then closed. He stepped quickly forward and kissed her.

From 'A Room with a View' by E. M. Forster (1879–1970)
English novelist and essayist

The Timeline

When I work on my novels, I rarely write the scenes in chronological order. However, when I'm ready to put everything together, I always create a timeline of my characters' lives for the duration of the novel. I think of this timeline as a kind of written meditation on behalf of my novel: an active attentiveness to the world I have created. This, of course, includes the seasons, and I often have to do a little rewriting when I find that I've made a day too warm or too light when it would actually be winter, or because I need to take traditional festivals or holidays into account. I always enjoy this rewriting, and I think the story is generally better shaped and becomes more real for the extra work.

I think of this timeline as a kind of written meditation on behalf of my novel

MINDFULNESS EXERCISE

SPARKING ORIGINALITY WITH THE SEASONS

Take a scene you have already written. This could be something that's really happened – an entry from your journal, perhaps – but you'll need to use your imagination. Now, reset the scene during a different season of the year and rewrite it. You might actually realize that your original scene doesn't involve a season at all, but could have taken place at any time. It will help you to engage better with your writing to decide on your character's reactions as she moves through her world or looks out of her window. A shiver, for example, not only shows your character responding to her surroundings but also presents a useful change of mood, which helps to create atmosphere.

Significant Change

The seasons teach us about change, and about expectation. In fiction writing, of course, the writer creates change for the characters in a story. In a novel, for instance, there will usually be many turns and changes between the beginning and end. In a short story, however, there would usually be only one significant change. The writing examples on the following pages illustrate the point.

Writing Example

Significant change is not the same as incident or event. Please read these two versions of the same story:

There is a bored housewife. She goes to buy some bread, giving a pound to a homeless beggar she sees on the street. The baker tells her about his son who is doing a sponsored walk. She waves to a friend across the street; goes home. Her life is so boring.

Events have happened – going to the shops, talking to the baker, waving to a friend, going home – but there have been no changes, not at least in a literary sense. But please consider the second version of this story:

There is a bored housewife. She goes to buy some bread, giving a pound to a homeless beggar she sees on the street. The baker tells her about his son who is doing a sponsored walk. She has an idea about raising funds for the homeless. She calls to a friend across the street, 'Would you like to join me on a sponsored walk?'

The same events have happened, but there has been a change in the mind of the main character. She sees her world differently. It's no longer boring but contains the anticipation of fulfilment.

Writing Example

Here is a short outline of a story (based on a traditional tale):

Thomas and Hassan are not very well off, but they are happy with their lives and glad to be best friends. They live on the coast and Thomas loves surfing, but in the winter the sea is too cold, and he would like to have a wetsuit so he can surf every day.

Hassan's hobby is riding his bicycle, but the roads are poor where they live, and full of ruts, and he often has to repair his tyres and wheels. He would like to have mountain-wheels fitted to his bicycle.

At the time of a gift-giving festival, Thomas sells his surfboard to buy mountain-wheels for Hassan who, in turn, sells his bike to buy a wetsuit for his friend.

Of course, this is only the 'bare bones' of the story. Interest and characterization would be added by the writer to give it life. But I think you will see 'the world of the story' initially as two boys with hobbies. By the end of the story, we see the depth of their friendship. For both boys, the other's happiness is more important than their own hobbies and interests.

If, instead, each of the boys had saved up enough money to buy what he wanted, although events would still have happened, there wouldn't have been the 'significant change' that revealed the story's message.

It is 'significant change' that reveals the point of our fictional stories, and a short story is sometimes defined as 'a moment of change'. Here is a basic structure on which to construct a short story:

• We see a fictional scenario or mood – the world of the story being lived or viewed in a certain way.

• There is a moment of change (this need not be at the end of the story).

• Finally, we see a new scenario or mood – the world of the story being lived or viewed differently because of what has happened.

This 'significant change' need not be in the life of the fictional characters, but rather in the mind of the reader. After all, in real life, we often mistake personalities or situations – perhaps thinking a cheerful person is happy when they are carrying some tragic problem; or seeing a plant as dead when it is dormant for the winter. The writer's job is to reveal the hidden interest in a story, which creates a satisfying 'change' for the reader.

DAY & NIGHT

Day and night are the very first of all things in the story of the creation of the universe. According to the Bible, God began by making two great lights, 'the greater light to rule the day and the lesser light to rule the night'.

THESE DIVISIONS BETWEEN LIGHT AND DARK are an absolutely normal and yet profound reality of our lives and the world we live in. Light is so uplifting, especially after a sleepless night, and yet darkness can be comforting and beautifully mysterious. One of my happiest nights was one I spent a few years ago, wrapped up in a warm coat and blankets in my back garden, viewing a total eclipse of the moon on a completely clear winter's night. It was wonderful for me to see the shadow of our own planet visibly moving slowly over the surface of the moon. It is a happy memory of a beautiful spectacle in which I felt I belonged. There was no point in it, no reason for it, but recalling that night reminds me that every experience of every day can be viewed with the same wonder and delight. Nothing needs a reason for its own beauty, its own wonder. Every day, every task can be viewed in this way.

darkness can be comforting and beautifully mysterious

Our writing is an extension of our thoughts. Some people (you and me, for example) feel the need to write.

We don't have to excuse ourselves. Do we expect a lark to provide an excuse for its ecstatic song? We don't need to prove anything. But a lark's task is to sing; and our task is to write. It may sometimes seem difficult, but the difficulty can be approached with a peaceful mind. The task of writing can be seen as a cycle of day and night. When the time seems right and we can write easily, that is the daytime of our writing. When it feels more difficult, we can take the opportunity to watch out the time with mindfulness meditation, as we can watch the moon and stars at night – a pause to recognize with awareness our own beauty, our own potential for creativity.

The task of writing can be seen as a cycle of day and night

Daydreams

Undoubtedly, all writers begin as daydreamers. At school, my teachers often accused me of 'dreaming' when I should have been attending to the class subject. It was true! While sitting at my desk I was off travelling to magical lands on winged horses, rescuing loved ones from thrillingly perilous situations, or on some other adventurous quest far from the classroom. Eventually, I suppressed the dreaming and tried to concentrate on ordinary life: passing exams, obtaining a job, building relationships. But mindfulness has taught me that my daydreams are just as valuable as ordinary life. They are part

MINDFULNESS EXERCISE

A 'WRITING-YOUR-DAYDREAMS' MEDITATION

- You will need your writing materials. You will also need those few 'waiting to write' meditative moments, as before. So sit comfortably, close your eyes and bring your attention to your breath. Sit and breathe with awareness for some minutes. When you feel relaxed, allow the subject of daydreams to come into your mind.
- Now, take a sheet of paper and write a list of any daydreams that you can remember, from your earliest childhood to your very latest ones. This should be written quickly, as with our previous list-writing exercise, without judgement or analysis. Just a few words for every daydream.
- Next, review your list and choose one daydream. Use this for a page or two of writing, taking the essence of the original idea and adding anything you wish. Who is your central character? Where is she? What is the direction of her life and how is it to change?

This could be the start of a great new story!

of me and can be accepted mindfully, enjoyed and incorporated into my writing life.

If you have been accused of 'dreaming', that's great. You are halfway to being a writer without even picking up your pen.

Night-dreams

When they sleep, some people have very vivid dreams. Do you ever wonder at the meaning of a dream, and feel it might be in need of interpretation?

Psychology in many worldwide traditions includes dream interpretation. In modern Western psychology, the most famous interpreter of dreams was Sigmund Freud, who saw a connection between people's dreams and their mental and psychological state. Joseph Campbell's later work on myth and story expanded some of Freud's ideas into the realms of collective consciousness. Campbell saw ancient spiritual and religious traditional stories as being directly connected with the psychology of the times.

Personally, I like the idea of connecting dreams with stories. In one of my most memorable and lovely night-dreams, I was with a group of people and we were diving from the land into a deep and beautiful blue pool, where we would swim underwater for a long time. In the dream, I felt entirely relaxed and happy; I could breathe under the water with perfect ease. From this dream came the inspiration for a short story, *Everest Island*. But I never really tried to interpret the dream. It seemed to have no bearing on any of

I like the idea of connecting dreams with stories

SIT WITH YOUR DREAM

If you have made some notes about a dream, sit with the notes and spend some time in mindful awareness. Beginning with breathing, introduce to your mind the way you feel about the dream. Perhaps it was disturbing, intriguing, delightful; just be aware of that emotion, without any judgement or analysis. Simply sit with the feeling for a while. Later, let your notes guide your writing. You can try interpreting the dream if you wish, or perhaps just use it to inspire a new story or poem.

my waking experiences at that time; I was only glad of the joyful sensation it brought with it.

Because dreams can feed the imagination so vividly with visions and ideas, and yet quickly fade as the waking world takes over, why not keep a notebook and pencil beside you when you sleep? On waking, you can jot down the gist of any dreams that you remember. These notes will help to keep your dreams alive and will become an inspirational resource for your writing.

CHAPTER THREE

Good Practice

Through mindfulness, every writer can reach a deep creative awareness beyond ordinary thoughts and everyday concerns. When we tap into that awareness, we write easily and without noticing the passing of time. That is the sought-after writing experience we would all hope to attain, and I believe this can happen for any of us. But, ideally, the resultant writing will be accessible, articulate and enjoyable for the reader. In this chapter, we consider ways for the writer to prepare, so when we touch that deep creative awareness, our writing will be the very best it can be.

Mindfulness, A Commitment to Yourself

Before beginning any task, I need to remember mindfulness. Everything I have ever been, or I have known, learned, experienced, comes together in this one present moment. I believe mindfulness helps me to be the best I can, including being the best writer I can.

SOMEONE ONCE SAID TO ME, 'But won't mindfulness meditation cause you to be so content with your life that you won't have the ambition to write any more?' I had to think about this, and the true answer was 'I don't know'. I was fairly new to meditation at the time, and it was helping me with my life to an almost unbelievable extent. My relationships, working life, recreational activities, all were becoming easier and more enjoyable. Nothing was perfect, of course – it never is. But my problems had eased, angst reduced and happiness increased since beginning mindfulness meditation. So, even for the sake of my writing, I was not prepared to give it up.

However, as I mentioned in the introduction to this book, my writing life really began simultaneously with my meditation practice. Writing no longer seemed an insurmountable challenge, beyond my ability. I became happy to write with intention but without the stressful pressure of ambition, and I was able to take advantage of opportunities as they came to me. That's why I have faith in mindfulness; simply because it works for

me. It isn't a case of banishing ambition, but of noticing it with a smile and returning my attention to my writing.

Yes, there have been times when what seemed greater priorities might have caused my meditation practice to lapse for a while. And, yes, it has sometimes been difficult to take it up again. Why this difficulty happens is a mystery, but other people have said the same. It's as if the ego takes hold and is reluctant to let go of our lives. But with determination to spend time in present-moment awareness and a few minutes' mindful breathing every day, meditative practice returns with all its gentle benefits. That is why I decided to begin this chapter on 'good practice' with mindfulness. It's because I believe that, more than anything else, it can enhance all the other practices that help improve the quality of our writing lives.

A New Country for the Mind

People who practise mindfulness meditation regularly find it easier to take time out for a little present-moment awareness during their daily lives. Even in an important meeting, a few seconds' grounding on the floor beneath your feet, noticing your breathing, mindful of the surface texture of a desk under your hand, can restore a sense of calm in a stressful situation.

In order to have the skill to 'call up' mindfulness at will, even at the most difficult moments, it's an idea to devote time to mindfulness alone. This is when we try to quiet the 'self-talk' inside our minds. For a writer, this is particularly important.

Because we work with words all the time, we need to unravel the jumble of words in our minds in order to use them with perception later. Far from making our minds 'go blank', this is an adventurous activity, like discovering a new country; we are forming a space into which we can bring our creativity. By living adventurously, we can turn away from all our activities for a certain time every day and give that time to settling our minds. In this way, we can return to our writing fresh in mind.

Defragmenting the Mind

When I had my first computer, I was advised to 'defragment' it regularly. Very soon, I realized that 'defragmenting' was a kind of meditation for my computer. All the particles of data that were slightly out of place returned to their proper position during the process, and the computer was quicker and more accurate afterwards. I only had to invite the computer to perform the defragmentation by pressing the correct button. That is what we are doing with meditation: inviting the mind to return its various parts to their proper, peaceful state, so that our minds become calmer, more able to deal with life and – hopefully – quicker and more accurate too.

At this time in my life, I meditate for at least thirty minutes each day, and twice a day is ideal for me. During meditation problems and frustrations begin to dissolve. I notice them with awareness, mindful of the way they make me feel. Without judgement, I sit with them – not thinking, just perceiving my feeling, often using an affirmation such as 'I am peaceful'. Usually I find that even the most difficult dilemmas, sadnesses and troubles become easier to cope with. It doesn't always happen quickly; I have had to come back to certain problems, time after time, and sit with the way they feel until my mind is settled.

Problems with writing can be dealt with mindfully in the same way as personal problems. It isn't a case of sitting and puzzling out practicalities or plot layout. We are sitting with a view to settling our minds.

THE WRITER'S SANGHA

To practising Buddhists, a sangha is a community of scholars and practitioners who support each other locally and internationally. This is considered to be of such importance that the sangha is one of the Three Jewels of Buddhist teaching: Buddha, Dharma and Sangha.

MANY BUDDHISTS HAVE PRACTISED ALONE when they have been isolated, exiled or even imprisoned. At such times, spiritual practice has sustained them. But there is nothing so good as having one's spiritual friends nearby, being able to contact them and share thoughts, problems and joys. Most people who have meditated in a group have noticed the potent atmosphere generated by several people sitting together in silence. As well as Buddhists and others, this is also true of Quakers who meet in silence every week. On a personal level,

MINDFULNESS EXERCISE

BEGINNING MEDITATION AGAIN

You might like to try this whether you are a meditation beginner or coming back to it after a break. The idea is to be gentle with yourself and not expect too much at the start.

- Ideally, go into a room where you can be alone for a while and close the door. Sit comfortably, but don't spend too much time getting comfortable. The ego is always keen to tell us we are not ready for meditation.
- Some people light a candle and focus on the flame during meditation. Others use incense or aromatic oils. Gentle music can be helpful, but it doesn't suit everyone. Choose your own way of creating a calm space. However, don't spend too much time preparing.
- You might feel an almost unbearable restlessness. If so, acknowledge this restlessness. Make a deal with it. Just one minute's mindfulness meditation and you can stop.
- Set a timer to ring after a minute. Close your eyes. As before, notice your breathing, and be aware of the temperature of the air as it enters and leaves your body. Notice any thoughts, notice your restlessness, and then return your attention to your breath. It can help to use an affirmation, saying words such as 'I breathe in peace,

I breathe out calm', either aloud or as a silent thought, while breathing mindfully. Affirmations like this can be powerful anti-stress remedies.

- When the timer has gone off, try again, this time for two minutes or perhaps longer – say five minutes. When I am feeling restless, I find it particularly beneficial to notice the quality of my impatience, irritation or boredom. Notice it without judgement or analysis, and return the attention to the breathing. Use the word 'Peace' with the in-breath, 'Calm' with the out-breath. I might feel physically uncomfortable in some way. Perhaps my nose starts itching. I acknowledge the itch and turn my attention back to my breathing.
- If you have managed this for five minutes, that is a very good start. Next time you could try it for longer. But don't expect too much of yourself. The ego can be like a sore heel or fractious child. It needs treating gently. At first, or during times of great busyness, it is better to sit mindfully for five minutes every couple of hours than to attempt a thirty-minute meditation when your mind is full of stress and anxiety. And, in my experience, short sessions accumulate, resulting in a calmer mind.

I find concentration so much easier within a group, and meditation more powerful and beneficial.

It's the same with writing, which is usually a solitary occupation and can make us feel lonely. If we have an editor, publisher and/or agent, they provide most valuable support and encouragement for our writing practice. However, few of us have been able to establish such a professional relationship, especially when we begin writing. So I would recommend that you find a 'writing sangha': that is, a group of like-minded writers who support and inspire each other. This might involve trying a few groups before settling on the right one.

To Share or Not to Share

To have regular contact with a group of writing friends can be a blessing. That's how it is for me, and I've been a member of several writing groups in the past, which have all worked in different ways. One of them (which I still belong to) sets 'homework' and we all bring a short piece of work to read at the next meeting. This is good for me, as it's an opportunity to write something completely different from whatever my present book-writing project might be. I am a 'people person'; I love meeting up with others, so having that connection with a writing group is a pleasure in itself. But it isn't just a social matter for me. I am really grateful for the inspiration the group gives to me, and for the chance to practise the different methods of writing that this offers.

MINDFULNESS EXERCISE

FINDING A WRITING SANGHA

- For this exercise, I suggest that, choosing mindfully, you select a sheet of paper and a pen. Then please get comfortable, close your eyes and turn your attention to your breathing. Be aware of any thoughts but allow them to pass, and return to the breath. Again, perhaps using the word 'Peace' for the in-breath and 'Calm' for the out-breath, begin to settle your mind.
- After a few minutes, gently open your eyes. Now, begin to make some notes regarding your hopes and expectations of a 'writing sangha'. What advice would you like, if any? How much input would you be prepared to give to others? How do you think such a group might be run? Can you find out if there is one nearby? If there is nothing in your area, would you be able to travel? Could you start a group yourself? Do you know anyone you would invite to join? How much work would you be prepared to put into this? Would you prefer a face-to-face or online group? How will you go about finding out what's available?
- When you have made a few notes, put your pen down and sit back. Take a few more minutes sitting in mindful meditation. Be aware of your thoughts, but don't allow them to take hold; just settle your mind, then open your eyes and return to your page of notes. Do any of them stand out now as being something that could bring greater happiness to your writing practice? Because your written thoughts have been produced between two 'layers' of meditation, this will help you to have a more perceptive awareness of your own needs. Beyond ego or ambition, meditation helps us to know our true minds.

Some of the most beneficial 'writing sanghas' I've been part of were very small groups of two or three writers. In these groups, we take a close interest in each other's work, reading, discussing, making suggestions. There is a lot of trust and good feeling between us. I still have two close 'writing sangha' friends. I respect and value their input very highly, and feel a strong interest in the creation and success of their own work.

It could be that you would rather not share your writing. Even so, some input from others is likely to be a big help to most of us, so you could consider viewing an online site or writer's blog. There are many excellent writing communities online that could be worth trying. I belonged to one previously, and members read sections of each other's work and wrote reviews and suggestions. Some of the comments were more useful than others but, on the whole, I did find it helpful and encouraging.

Falling in Love with Words

A great treasure house of continually evolving language is open to us. As our individual bodies rely on the air that is shared with every other human being, so our creative writing feeds off a sustaining language, available to all. To receive this mindfully, like breathing mindfully, is a joyful practice.

Words are not just signposts to our thoughts. As writers, we belong to a creative dynasty that goes back to the beginnings of human society. When human beings began to form speech, they made sounds to create names and convey messages. I do not believe that these first words were chosen lightly, but with a sense of responsibility and an instinctive awareness or vibration that tried to match sound with concept. When we became more articulate, the storyteller would have been a valued member of society, travelling, bringing news, giving names to emotions, actions and phenomena; names that the listeners might have been hearing for the first time. Thus, language grew, connecting people with each other. A good story would have been told with rhythm, pace and feeling – as it still is today. Rhyming stories were enjoyed – and both rhythm and rhyme have always helped people remember a sequence of words. Eventually, stories and messages were written, but only a privileged few learned to read and write. This skill made them powerful.

It is worth remembering that there is still much power in the written word. Perhaps this is true today more than ever before, now that our words can be sent around the globe in the blink of an eye. Because of this, writers want to express themselves as clearly, eloquently and originally as they can. So, if you haven't done so already, this is the time to embark on a love affair with words.

The Magic of Love & Language

When did you last fall in love? How did that feel? It's an experience that usually begins with a glimpse of someone we find appealing and often some reciprocal glance of understanding that is affecting beyond logic and seems almost magical. So, after the initial thrilling moment, we strive to develop a relationship with the object of our infatuation and, while that (irrational) feeling lasts, he becomes the most fascinating subject on the planet. We develop a mental map detailing every one of the loved one's features, tone of voice, preferences, family background, hair colour, shoe size, pretty much everything.

We can use the pattern of falling in love as we cultivate a relationship with words: pursue them with fascination and appreciation; become an expert in their nuances of meaning and effect, use them with delight and love. Begin to expand your vocabulary. This is where a traditional dictionary wins over computer spellcheckers. As we flip through the pages, seeking a word meaning or spelling, unlooked-for words catch our attention. But, for the purpose of your new love affair, allow yourself to be distracted. In fact, I suggest that you actually let your fingers and eyes go for a stroll in a dictionary. Choose a page at random and find a word you haven't heard of. Try to write a sentence containing this word, ensuring you use its meaning correctly. Is there some other way you could express the meaning of that same sentence? Try rewriting it in a different way, changing some of the words.

The Sound of Words

Buy or borrow a book of poems, or find some online and print them out. Look at the shape of them on the page. Read them aloud, feeling the rhythm and rhyming of the words in your mouth. Look for alliteration and assonance. Write a sentence of your own using these poetic devices.

When you are reading, watch out for sentences that chime with resonance. There are different ways of expressing certain moods. Think about the way a word sounds – beyond its meaning. The words 'shriek' and 'shout' have very similar meanings, but the former has a sharper vowel sound. Choosing one or the other in a sentence would affect the atmosphere of a scene, because of the way the words sound, in the same way that someone's tone of voice can affect how we feel about what they say to us.

Using Language Mindfully

Choosing just the right words and formation of a sentence is an opportunity for mindfulness. With awareness of what you wish to express in words, and the mood or atmosphere you want to create, write with more intuition than logic. Then test it by reading aloud. Does this feel right? If one of the words seems to be out of accord with the impression you are attempting to convey, then try to find other words with similar meanings but a different tone. Practising in this way is good fun and will hone our writing skills to great effect.

Over the years I have collected a whole shelf full of books to help me with my writing. I have several dictionaries, books on English usage, grammar, punctuation, quotations, foreign words and phrases, name meanings, a rhyming dictionary, a collection of synonyms and antonyms, and – almost as valuable as my dictionaries – a large thesaurus. It would be very expensive to buy all of these at once, but, beginning with a dictionary, why not start a collection if you can? Many books can be bought second-hand, and much of the information found in them can also be obtained in libraries or online.

Reading Practice

It is essential for a writer to also be a reader. For most of us, this is a delightful task. We know our reading preferences, and the books we love to read usually steer us to the kind of writing we naturally want to do. This is not always so; a writer of crime fiction might relax by reading romance or biography. Even so, that writer will have completely immersed himself in the genre of crime fiction before attempting to write his first novel.

I can feel overwhelmed in a bookshop or library full of reading treasure. Because of that, I really love it when people recommend books for me to read. This takes me away from authors and genres I am used to, sending me off in different directions to new favourites. As I read, I am adding to my storehouse of words, and learning how other writers create story and atmosphere in ways that are impressive and inspiring.

To say I am fond of poetry would be an understatement. I suppose poetry is like the secret, passionate affair in this love story of words. Poetry is a major literary genre in itself, with many subgenres and important 'movements'. For anyone who likes to write poetry I make a plea: do please read poems too. Go to a bookshop or library and pick up a book of poems by someone you've never heard of. Open it at random and read a verse or two. If this doesn't appeal, try another book until you find something resonates with you. For me, there is nothing more contagious than reading poetry. Whenever I read it, I'm writing it very soon afterwards. It might not be the same for you, but I do believe that trying to write poetry is very good for our writing generally. Because many forms of poetry require certain patterns of syllables, metre, rhyme and so on, it gives our writing a work-out, and even if we don't feel our completed poem is very successful, it will have been an exercise in expression, which can only add to our overall writing skill.

THE CHALICE

At some point in the creation of a book, the writer will need to consider structure, so that all the features of the work hold together satisfactorily. With mindful awareness, structure becomes a valuable part of the creative process, like a beautiful chalice, perfectly containing our writing.

AN AUTHOR FRIEND OF MINE, Paul Fletcher, who has written and edited many books for the Chalice Well Press, told me that he approaches his writing in a meditative way. He sometimes sees the whole work as a 'chalice', encompassing the structure of the book, the research and study he has undertaken, and the deep connection he feels with the subject.

As Paul was speaking, I visualized an actual chalice cup, brimming with fascinating information and spiritual inspiration, yet perfectly contained within its own structure.

Before he writes, Paul always meditates. Then, he can 'just tune in' and the writing comes. But, he says, this is not any kind of 'channelling' but preparing oneself to be open to the creative spirit. And it occurred to me that the preparation Paul has done, including years of study and research, enables him to 'tune in' to a very rich source of information. Similarly, his years of regular writing practice enable what seems effortlessly well-written text.

Knowing him as a very spiritual, meditative man, I was almost surprised at Paul's enthusiasm for planning the struc-

---

There was a sense of Presence in the room that offered clarity, love and understanding to the work.

FROM 'LIGHT UPON THE PATH: THE UNPUBLISHED WRITINGS OF WELLESLEY TUDOR POLE'
BY PAUL FLETCHER, TRUSTEE OF THE CHALICE WELL AND CURATOR OF THE CHALICE WELL ARCHIVE

---

ture of his books. Yet structure is, of course, an integral aspect of written work, without which the most beautiful prose and absorbing information would fall apart. To be able to embrace joyfully this very practical aspect of writing serves our purpose well and brings great satisfaction.

The Framework

If we are just writing for ourselves, or to improve our written expression generally, we might not need to concern ourselves with the structure of the work. But for stories, biography, self-help guides or any other form of book or complete written work, we need to at some time plan a framework.

When I write my novels, I generally start at the beginning of the story with what I hope is an appealing opening to hold a reader's attention. Then, very soon afterwards, I write the last page. This is a great help to me, as, from then on, I always know where my story is heading. This is a real, if skeletal, structure for my novel. After that, I write chapters, often in no order at all. This usually depends on any research I've been undertaking for the project. I need to be aware that research should always be done on behalf of the characters in the story and never be put in for its own sake, no matter how interesting it is. Mindfulness helps me here; as I quietly consider the personalities and lives of my characters, I will know instinctively what aspects of my research will be relevant to the story. This helps me to write the scene with authenticity.

Constructing the Narrative

At some point, though, I need to organize the book's internal structure, including the highs and lows of the experience of the characters. These would normally be ordered as: ambition, conflict, success, disappointment, encouragement, near-failure and eventual resolution. Such peaks and troughs should hold a reader's attention and may be repeated throughout the book, depending on the complexity of the plot. Additionally, I usually want my characters to experience internal transformation, as well as external achievement, in my stories. This is the kind of 'significant change' mentioned on pages 54–5.

I produce a timeline for each character, showing their actions and experiences in relation to the book's timescale. This activity always highlights any anomalies – perhaps showing two characters as meeting when, in fact, events have placed one of them on the other side of the world at that time. So now I have to do some rewriting, correcting mistakes or faults in the plot and ensuring 'peaks and troughs' follow a pattern I hope will retain a reader's interest. I always greatly enjoy this process.

Other writers plan their books tightly right from the beginning, even before they write a page. I would imagine that this would be particularly important with genre books such as crime fiction or modern romance, when it's usually essential that the story follows an expected trajectory. Planning ahead is also vital when writing biography, in which case I would begin with a timeline, making notes for information I already have

MINDFULNESS EXERCISE

PLANNING FOR FUN

- Take a pen and paper, or prepare your laptop or tablet. Again, allow yourself a few minutes' quiet mindfulness, remembering that this settles the mind into a clearer, brighter space for writing.
- Imagine a character, and write down the bare bones of their life: age, gender, name, situation in life, family, historical period and so forth. This really applies to biography as much as fiction.
- Now, make some notes to help shape this character's story. What's important to her? What does she want most in life? What stops her having it? Who can help? How would you show a first success? What happens to thwart this? How can she overcome such a setback? What dramatic event might precipitate total failure? How could the situation be resolved successfully and satisfactorily for this character?
- Try to answer these questions with mindful knowledge of your characters and other aspects of your story. Along with structural elements like timelines and research, this should provide a useful basic framework to help create a perfect 'chalice' for your work.

on the subject of the biography such as their date of birth, and making it clear where I need to undertake extra research.

Constructing the narrative of a story can be very rewarding as the structure of the work takes shape. This will carry the inspired action, characters and landscapes of your creative imagination and bring them to life in the minds of the readers.

CHAPTER FOUR

VOICES

At the heart of every writer is their personal 'inner voice', as distinctive as our own speaking voice, conveying elements of personality and qualities such as gentleness or urgency or authority. While accepting and cherishing this, we need to be aware that our writing is full of the countless sounds and tunes and tones of the imagination. We speak as omniscient narrators of god-like powers, or as weak and timid characters at the mercy of the writer's pen.

FINDING THE INNER VOICE

Voices develop throughout our lives, often affected by physical, sociological and personal circumstances. But, as writers, it is possible to step aside from past influences and, by listening deeply, find our authentic voice. This can be a joyful and liberating process.

AS I WAS GROWING UP, I absorbed manners and opinions from the people around me. Although I knew I was well loved, I developed admiration for a certain kind of cynical tone of voice sometimes used to judge others. I went through a stage when, with friends, such a tone was thought of as very clever and very funny, even though it might have been at the expense of people who did not deserve it.

There came a time when I no longer wished to use this 'cynical voice'.

Being female in the 1960s, 70s and 80s required a certain attitude or tone in order to conform. I tended to step back from my own talents or abilities, other than what were considered the traditional pursuits of women. I cultivated a 'womanly' voice.

It was a time of great advancement in feminism; an exciting time for some, but probably not for the majority, and certainly not for me. It wasn't until I studied feminism in the late 1980s and 90s that my eyes were opened to the way females and males in our society had adopted an unjust attitude to the role of women. This also helped me to understand how others, especially minority groups of all kinds, were often wrongly treated in our society. I learned to use a 'feminist' voice.

In the 1990s there was a great movement in personal development. At that time, I was lucky to come into contact with someone who helped me to come to terms with what I thought of as problems in the past. Through her, I learned to see these as steps along the path to understanding myself and others. My 'voice' began to have a 'transformational' tone.

Not long afterwards, I picked up that book on meditation, and my life began to change in a big way.

Be not afeard; the isle is full of noises,
Sounds and sweet airs, that give delight and hurt not.
Sometimes a thousand twangling instruments
Will hum about mine ears; and sometime voices,
That, if I then had wak'd after long sleep,
Will make me sleep again: and then, in dreaming,
The clouds methought would open and show riches
Ready to drop upon me; that, when I wak'd
I cried to dream again.

From 'The Tempest', Act 3, Scene 2,
by William Shakespeare (1564–1616)
English playwright and poet

MINDFULNESS EXERCISE

A MEDITATION FOR PICTURING YOUR VOICE

- Take a breath just as you are now. Concentrate for a moment on the in-breath, then the out-breath. Now, prepare for mindfulness meditation. Find a quiet space where you can be alone. Make it comfortable, but take your writing paper and pen with you.
- Close your eyes and breathe normally and gently, mindful of the way the air feels as it enters and leaves your body. It may help you relax if you say, silently or quietly, the words 'I breathe in peace; I breathe out calm'. After a few minutes, allow yourself to become aware of your own mental feelings and emotions. There may be a sense of deep peacefulness and happiness. There may be leftover positive or negative emotions of no great depth. If there is anger, despair, sadness, fear or other strong negative emotions, don't deny them, but sit with them, without judgement, as you would with a friend who needs you. This is no time for words or naming, no time for analysis or judgement. Look upon these emotions, and yourself, with the deepest compassion.
- After at least five minutes, open your eyes and prepare to write. Is there an imaginary or real place that you feel some longing for – a kind of home for the soul? Does some other image come to mind that seems to represent your deepest emotions – perhaps an animal, landscape, element or building? Listen deeply; write affectionately. There is no need for fear; be adventurous, like a traveller setting out willingly on a path to the future. If nothing comes to mind this time, or your writing doesn't quite connect with your inner voice, don't worry; you have begun a worthwhile inner journey, and can come back to this exercise whenever you wish.

Picturing the Voice

Since I was eight years old I had loved reading, and I admired writers so much that I always knew that writing was what I wanted to do. But, as an adult, I had no strong self-belief. Dreaming of success, ambitious without focus, I knew how to use 'cynical', 'womanly', 'feminist' and 'transformational' voices, but what of my own personal voice? Where was it, how could I find it, and did I want to? I was not at all sure that I was ready to look at what was deep within my being. In some ways, it frightened me.

It was while reading my journal, which I've been writing almost continually (but not always daily) since I was twelve years old, that I began to have an inkling of that inner voice. I noticed that my writing often had a cheerful and gentle tone, even at times of terrible sadness and anxiety. Reading my own words, I found encouragement and positivity in the last place I had expected to find it – in my own journal.

That was when I began to realize how meditation was leading me to look for my authentic inner voice. One day, I sat down and wrote about what I was trying to find. First, I described my inner voice as if it was a song. Then, an image came to me, and I wrote a description of a deep underground pool with its own integral light. Although rather surprising (because, actually, I don't like going underground), it seemed just the right image for my inner voice. To me, it was comforting, supportive and very peaceful, and I often find myself going back to it in times of stress. I believe that something of my true inner voice is reflected in this image, which seems to come from a place where mindfulness and the imagination meet.

Other Voices

While keeping a mindful awareness of our authentic inner voice, we can still develop the skills to 'speak' in different ways through our writing. Just as an actor cherishes her true identity while playing many parts, we can choose to use various 'voices' depending on our story and characters.

I was once told, 'Everyone has a recognizable "writer's voice", just like their spoken voice.' This surprised me and actually shook my confidence, as when I began to practise my writing, I would read the work of various authors I admired and try to emulate their style. This was a fascinating and enjoyable exercise, if not always successful. The writers included Shakespeare, Jane Austen, Virginia Woolf and several modern writers of many different styles. Was I being 'inauthentic' or dishonest in some way? But it occurred to me that it is actually necessary for a writer to be able to adjust the tone and style of her work. After all, two characters in a novel would be expected to have different ways of expressing themselves, just as people do in real life. If a writer

THE GOOD LISTENER

'Loving Speech and Deep Listening' is one of the Five Mindfulness Trainings taught by Zen Master Thich Nhat Hanh. Deep listening is a beautiful practice, helping us to understand others and live at peace. We can begin by employing deep listening in our approach to ourselves and our attitude towards our writing work. Do you have an ideal reader who would 'listen' attentively to your work?

I often think that my ideal reader would enjoy the same subjects that I do, and provide gentle advice and guidance while encouraging and spurring me on. Yes, she is perfect. But such a kind confidant is not so difficult to find. We have the potential to be our own guide and adviser.

Deep listening includes accepting all the uncertainties and difficulties that might occur while we are trying to write. Instead of berating ourselves for an uninteresting paragraph, we need to ask 'How could this be better?' If we feel unsure of grammar or punctuation, we can make a plan of action to improve in these areas. If we are tired, we can rest. All of this (yes, even the resting) can be done adventurously, with a positive mind, knowing that from self-acceptance comes the road to joyful intention. We need to understand our capabilities and not to expect too much. With small steps, our writing and our meditation can vastly improve, enhancing every area of our lives and helping us to use a similar, gentle manner in our approach to others.

So let us release any negative thoughts about our writing. Let our daily meditation contain a feeling of deep love for our creative work, as trusting and supporting as the love of a treasured grandparent.

was unable to put this across, then the story would be dull and monochromatic in tone.

I am glad now to have an image for my inner voice and, through my journal, an inkling of how it 'sounds' on the page. But when I'm writing fiction, articles or even poetry, I make deliberate choices about tone, pace and so forth, depending on what seems suitable for my purpose.

This is where mindfulness is a great help. My calm 'waiting to write' time before I begin helps to shape the space in which my creativity will become active. One of the benefits of this is that I develop an awareness of my hopes for the work – the personalities of characters, the setting, landscape and mood of the world I am creating. During meditation, I try not to articulate words for this. I am settling the mind, quietening the 'babble' of my own voice, and any 'voice of doubt' that might arise. From the silence will come my proper intention for the book, including voices that do not seem to be my own, but nonetheless come from my own imagination, experience and practise as a writer.

Narrative Tone

'Tone of voice' in writing doesn't only mean the tone of a speaking character. It also concerns the general mood of a particular scene or even a whole book. This is where the 'narrator' uses a voice that is not necessarily the inner voice of the writer. The writer can take on a narrative persona that is not their own. For example, when Daphne du Maurier writes at the beginning of *Rebecca*, 'Last night I dreamt I went to Manderley again', she is not writing as herself, but as the fictional character telling the story, the young Mrs de Winter.

Narrative tone can carry emotion, tension and atmosphere. The examples on page 92 are all possible first paragraphs for a story called *The Stable Yard*. Each has a different narrative tone; each could be memories of the central character. Whichever was chosen would set the tone for the whole story.

Listening, Toning, Tuning

Written words are silent, so the reader needs to be made aware of mood and atmosphere without the benefit of actually hearing the pitch and pace of your voice. But these can be expressed through writerly technique. Short phrases, for example, can tend to give an impression of urgency, while long, meandering sentences will usually create a more relaxed, tranquil mood.

When you are reading, 'listen' to the voice of the narrator. Are they trying to convey a certain atmosphere in their

---

A voice cannot carry the tongue and the
lips that gave it wings. Alone must it seek the ether.

FROM 'THE PROPHET', KAHLIL GIBRAN (1883–1931)
LEBANESE-AMERICAN POET

Writing Example

She was five years old when Grandad first put her on a horse. She sat there, engulfed in amazement, feeling a big smile stretching her face. Her fingers were hooked into the rough mane under her hands, and she was high above the world, carried by the heat and scent and sheer living hugeness of the horse.

When he was three, he was too big to sleep with Mum and Dad any more. So they gave him a room and a large, cold bed of his own. The room faced on to the stable yard and at night he could hear the bump and scrape of hooves and bodies moving about in the stalls.

Years later I returned again to Briar farm. A business trip had taken me to a town nearby and, on impulse, I turned left instead of right at the junction, drove for a hundred yards or so, and sat in the car for a long time, facing the old stable yard.

writing, or even trying to influence your opinion? If you think so, try to notice how this is achieved. In the pair of examples that follow, it's easy to see how the narrator might be trying to convey prejudice or sympathy:

That woman's stupid. She only wastes cash on beggars so she'll feel better about her own riches. But it's their choice. They should get a job and not bother decent people.

Leila was moved by the plight of the poor in her own district. She would give a coin to anyone she saw begging, and sometimes take food and sit with them, talking for a while.

Of course, the content of these two paragraphs indicate the opinion supposed to be expressed by the narrator. But the tone of voice also conveys a certain air of disgust in the first example and gentleness in the second.

Listen to your own inner thoughts and feelings. When journalling, aim to express these as closely as possible. But in writing practice, try different methods of writing a sentence to convey emotion or mood in various ways. Try also to write opinions that are not your own, and to make them convincing. Practising this will enable you to speak in the voice of any character in your story.

Creating Awareness for the Reader

When portraying a character or scene, it is neither necessary nor even desirable to describe every detail of the situation. It is possible to generate anticipation and curiosity in the

MINDFULNESS EXERCISE

A CHARACTERIZATION EXERCISE

- This exercise is to write a scene, showing a character's movements and reactions in such a way that the reader will be aware of their personality, mood and preoccupations.
- Gather your writing materials, pen, paper or keyboard. Before we begin, let's take a few minutes to settle the mind. I hope this is becoming second nature to you now! Close your eyes, notice your breathing. Don't let any thoughts take hold. For this 'waiting' time, acknowledge the thoughts and allow them to pass.
- After five minutes or so, open your eyes and begin. I want you to write a paragraph about a character going about an everyday task. This might be driving a car, making breakfast or working. Try to create an awareness of the character's mood, state of mind and personality based on the way they move, act and speak. This is a good way to start feeling comfortable with a variety of 'narrative voices'.

reader by holding back on information, while allowing an awareness of action, emotion and personality. Rather than saying that a character is, for example, 'messy', 'meticulous', 'unwell', 'excited', 'unhappy', 'in love' and so on, it is far more interesting to show them reacting to aspects of their world in such a way that shows their personality. In the example on the facing page, the character, Sally, is waking up in the morning and making breakfast.

Writing Example

The alarm beeped just once before Sally's hand silenced it. After a quick shower, she dressed carefully in her new suit. Unable to face her usual breakfast, she put a single slice of bread in the toaster and clicked on the kettle. Her eyes turned to the neat pile of papers beside her handbag. Everything was ready. She spread her single slice of toast thinly with butter, taking a bite and a sip of tea, then checking the papers again before folding them into her bag. Trembling a little in the new suit, she checked her appearance in the mirror, took a deep breath and left the apartment.

It seems that Sally has some significant appointment this morning. Without being told what this is, or even how she feels, the reader is still aware that Sally is experiencing tension and nervousness as she prepares for her day.

Of course, there are times when we need to use words of explanation such as 'nervous' or 'hungry', but we also want to let the reader enter the world we are creating with our writing, and experience for themselves the characters' movements and reactions.

LISTENING TO YOUR CHARACTERS' VOICES

Writers often feel very close to the fictional characters they are creating. Almost as much as real friends, they will enjoy getting to know the background, personalities and voices of these people inhabiting an imaginary existence. This level of familiarity also lends an impression of authenticity to the writing.

DO IDEAS FOR CREATIVE WRITING ever come 'out of the blue', when the writer is not expecting anything of the sort? I do think it is possible that there are moments when we are especially receptive to the life of the imagination. My belief is that this is more likely to happen if we are practising writers who regularly allow mindfulness to clear a space of creativity in our minds.

My most successful fictional character appeared quite unexpectedly. One Wednesday morning some years ago I attended a regular meditation session with friends. We were chatting afterwards, and my friend June showed us some new cards she had just received. On one side of each card was a picture of an animal, and on the reverse was information about the animal and its natural and mythological connections. As I got up to leave, I looked down at the cards and one of them attracted my attention. It had a picture of a deer on the front. I have no particular affinity with deer, but I asked June if I could borrow the card, and she readily agreed.

A Novel is Born

To this day I still have no idea why I felt the urge to borrow that card, but when I arrived home, I sat down on my stairs and straight away read the text on the back of the card. Under the mythological section it stated that, in the stories of King Arthur, Sir Gawain followed a white deer into the forest. The stories of King Arthur are traditional stories of a mythological English king and his Knights of the Round Table. The 'Round Table' was the king's way of abolishing hierarchy. Every knight, and the king himself, had equal status around that table.

As I sat on the stairs, reading the card, a story came immediately into my mind about a woman who lived in the time of King Arthur and wanted to be a knight.

I couldn't wait. I climbed the stairs to my little writing room and began to write a short story. I still have the original manuscript. When I'd finished, I entered it for a competition and it won. But the main character in that short story wouldn't leave my imagination. One day, I asked her a question, 'What was your first memory?'

She answered, 'What I remember is this …'.

Conversations with My Character

That was the beginning of a relationship that closed happily with the completion of a second novel. Many times during the writing of those two books, I paused to have a 'conversation'

MINDFULNESS EXERCISE

WRITING A MINDFUL CONVERSATION

Try this with a fictional character you have created.

- Choosing mindfully, select two pens of different coloured ink and some paper. You might like to keep a special notebook just for this purpose. Sitting comfortably, with your back straight if possible, close your eyes and breathe mindfully, noticing, as usual, the feeling of the air as you breathe in and out. You may already have some ideas for this exercise but, for this important time, don't give any attention to them. This is your 'waiting to write' time; for settling and clearing creative space in the mind.
- When you are ready, open your eyes and take up the pen you have chosen for your own voice. Now, 'look for' your character in writing. He might be clearly before you straight away, in the front of your mind, or you may have to write a little before you can see him properly. When you feel you have his attention, begin the conversation. There could be some detail of his life that is indistinct to you, or you may want to ask him what he feels about some specific incident in the story. Remember to use a different colour pen for his voice; this gives a useful pause between his voice and your own.

Don't be surprised if entirely unexpected ideas come from this exercise. The mind is a wonderful thing.

with that character, whose name is Edith. It was always a written conversation, and it always took place in a meditative way. I would choose two pens of different colours, one for me and one for my imaginary character, and keep a particular notebook for these 'conversations'.

At one time, I had been feeling 'blocked'. What I was writing seemed inauthentic somehow and I couldn't get on with the story. It was time to speak to Edith.

I took my special notebook and two pens, and sat quietly, breathing mindfully. I quickly noticed the feeling of frustration with my writing but, trying not to judge it or let it take hold, I 'waited to write', clearing the creative space in my mind. Then, I looked for Edith and began the written conversation. It quickly became clear that my frustration was also hers. I had forced a character (her father) to take action that was actually entirely inappropriate for his personality. 'My father would never do that!', she said. Because of my mistake, of course the other characters couldn't react well towards him, nor could the rest of the story work properly. Once I had realized this, a considerable amount of rewriting was required, but I didn't mind; I was happy that the 'block' had shifted.

I would choose two pens of different colours, one for me and one for my imaginary character

SPEAKING OUT

While it is important to be able to 'speak' in various moods and tones of voice, depending on the personality of a fictional character, when we speak out for a cause, or give expression to silent emotions, it's our personal inner voice that comes to the fore.

COMPASSION IS AN IMPORTANT aspect of Buddhist teaching. It is based on accepting that everyone, including ourselves, needs happiness and has the right to overcome suffering. When we feel moved by the plight of others, we can use our skills as writers to support a good cause or illuminate the lives of those who suffer. This is a way of living compassionately.

Sometimes we feel strongly about some issue or situation that seems unjust, unfair or simply wrong, but there seems to be nothing we can do. We may not have the strength, ability, time or confidence to fly out and help the victims of disasters, discover a cure for disease, or march in support of a cause. The world has so many ethical and social problems, no individual can change everything. This is where our mindfulness and our writing can give us power we might not have thought of.

Understanding Ourselves

In our 'waiting to write' times, we are practising being fully aware of the present moment and of our true intention for our writing. Making a regular habit of such meditative practice also helps us to understand ourselves, what our real interests and abilities are, and any areas where we feel we might need to change.

After I had been meditating regularly for some time, I began to notice the quality of my own level of attention when exposed to various subjects, not only during writing or reading times, but also when watching TV, listening to the radio, or even hearing conversation. When something truly interested me, I became still, focused, unlikely to be distracted. Noticing my own reactions mindfully made me aware that some subjects and issues I tried to take an interest in were not really suited to my character and abilities. Social or intellectual pressure might have made me feel that I should give my time to, for example, certain acclaimed literary works or sporting activities, but they didn't really hold any strong interest for me. Because of that, I was not very good at writing about them. This understanding was quite liberating!

Write About What You Love

I discovered that other subjects were fascinating and easily held my concentration. For me these included spirituality, mental health, history, nutrition, education. Because I seemed to absorb information on these subjects without effort, they were easy (and enjoyable) for me to address in my writing. Keeping to the areas I love also means research is much more appealing and rewarding, because I am studying what truly interests me.

Begin to notice your true interests. If you become aware of your attention being pulled towards certain subjects, then (if you don't do so already) bring them into your writing practice. Of course, your preferences will probably not be the same as mine. We are all unique, and our writing is supposed to be joyful for us. Let's therefore write about what we love. This, of course, might not necessarily be cheerful, but to draw the attention of readers to the causes close to our hearts is rewarding in itself.

The Mindful Message

I have often been asked, 'What is the plot of a story? What does "plot" mean?' But I believe that the theme of a story is a more vital consideration for a writer. The theme is the underlying meaning or message of a story; the plot is what actually happens – how that underlying meaning is illustrated.

The theme of Shakespeare's *Romeo and Juliet* is 'the tragedy of mismatched love'. The plot is: boy meets girl, they fall in love, are thwarted by circumstances and die.

Plot and theme are very closely connected, and it's difficult to imagine Shakespeare planning *Romeo and Juliet* without deciding on the underlying meaning of the story first. But we really do not have to concern ourselves too much with technical words like 'plot' and 'theme' in order to write.

Is there something you want to say – a dearly held belief or topic that you find absorbing, and you wish to share with readers? This could form the underlying meaning, message or theme of your work. Some of the themes that fascinate me include forgiveness, redemption and human love beyond romantic or family bonds. Other writers choose themes that are quite different, yet equally central to human existence. For example, Nick Hornby's *Fever Pitch* deals with the collective passion at the core of football. When I read it, I came to understand as never before the peaks and troughs of my family's reactions to the fortunes of their team. Beyond this, the book also seems to contain a profound message about loyalty in human nature.

Speaking Your Mind

Because we are writers, if we feel strongly about something, whether it is an international issue or an entirely personal concern, it's natural for us to want to put our feelings into writing. Whether or not this is ever read by anyone, we need to voice our thoughts and emotions.

In one of my creative writing classes, I would encourage students to write a letter to a newspaper, giving their opinion about any news item. Not everyone wanted their words made public, but many were happy to do so. Several of those letters did appear in print, and some of them were quite passionately expressed. My students could proudly announce that they were published writers! It was a good way to begin to articulate their thoughts and try out their powers of persuasion.

The Unsent Letter

Another class activity, intended to help with tuning in to our true thoughts, was to write a letter to someone in our life whom for some reason we cannot talk to. This could, for example, be a loved one who has died, or anyone distant or unavailable. I once did an exercise like this for myself, writing to a young man who had spoken to me sympathetically when I was in hospital as a child. Although this happened many years ago, I wanted to say how his kindness had made a real difference to that little girl. I never knew his name or anything about him, so although I couldn't send the letter I was able to express my gratitude, and explain how I had learned that day the importance of kindness to strangers.

The second part of the activity involves writing in the 'voice' of the other person, seeing situations from their point of view. Such an exercise is good for exercising the imagination. It can also cultivate compassion in the mind and help to dispel negative emotions such as anger by developing an understanding awareness of how the experience could have felt for the other person.

I was able to express my gratitude

In our writing life, we deal with many subjects close to our hearts. Through mindful awareness we can learn to tune in to the countless voices of the imagination, which will enhance our understanding and help us to live compassionately through our writing.

MINDFULNESS EXERCISE

THE COMPASSIONATE CONVERSATION

This exercise, as described on the facing page, will be to write to someone who is missing in your life, or who you would like to talk with but for some reason cannot do so. Although the writing will be in the form of a letter, it is not intended that you should send it.

- Choosing a pen and paper, sit comfortably and prepare for a short session of mindful awareness. Close your eyes, as usual, and notice your breathing for a few minutes, perhaps using the word 'Peace' for the in-breath and 'Calm' for the out-breath. Although you might already know to whom you will address your letter, do not give your thoughts any attention for now, simply acknowledging them and returning your attention to the breath.
- When you feel relaxed and your mind is settled, begin to write your letter:

  'Dear …'

  Remembering what you wish to say, try to articulate your feelings as clearly as possible.

When you have finished, pause for a few minutes with mindful breathing, and then prepare to write another letter, this time from the other person to yourself. Before you begin, I suggest another few minutes of mindful awareness. As you write, try to put yourself into the mind of the other person and write with compassion.

CHAPTER FIVE

IMAGINE

The writer's mind has an infinite capacity for imagination. If we wish, we can fly with the eagle to its heady mountain eyrie, or creep through the eye of a needle beside a microscopic organism. In a heartbeat, we enter the minds of saints and despots, elephants and emperors, and see the world through their eyes. Imagination breaks the bounds of Earth and space, taking us to distant worlds. Imagining mindfully, we may infuse our writing with colour, drama and originality, so that the characters and landscapes we describe seem to spring from the page with life of their own.

MINDFULNESS AND IMAGINATION

Mindfulness is by no means 'nothingness' but a deeply profound awareness, which helps to control the mind and allows a more attentive access to our knowledge, experiences and emotions. All of these feed the writer's imagination, imparting originality and creativity to our work.

A FRIEND SUGGESTED THAT MINDFULNESS could be at odds with the active imaginative processes required for writing. But present moment awareness also includes understanding the way we think. Watching our minds helps us to know ourselves and how our memories, reactions and imaginations work, so that they will feed our creativity as writers. Such self-awareness also helps to reduce any prejudices or narrow thinking processes we may have accumulated in our lives, which can be stumbling blocks to creativity.

I had such a stumbling block some time ago when, for a while, I had been deeply despondent with my writing. So I decided to sit quietly and mindfully with the feeling, trying

Watching our minds helps us to know ourselves and how our memories, reactions and imaginations work

to be aware of it without judgement. Quite soon, I realized the source of my despondency was an obsolete belief that, because I could never be the world's best writer, then my work would always be worthless.

This ego-based belief went back years to a time when I had believed myself to be a 'perfectionist' and didn't think anything worthwhile unless it was the best of its kind. I knew very well that 'perfectionism' sets us up for failure even before we begin. So I smiled at my ego, and smiled at my despondency. Understanding this aspect of myself, I was able to happily write again, without needing to be the best writer in the world.

Knowing Ourselves

If we learn to watch our minds, it can help us to understand the 'shape' of certain emotions such as anger. Watching ourselves mindfully when we are angry not only helps to control the anger itself, but also allows us to stand far enough back from the emotion and its causes as to be able to describe the experience in writing.

Being watchful is not the same as inactivity. If we witness injustice or cruelty and feel angry, we need not react to the anger, but we can still do our best to assist a victim. Other feelings – excitement, boredom, admiration, shame, pity, envy – the list goes on, but they can all be understood through mindfulness and, for the writer, be fuel for our imagination.

BEGINNING AS A CHILD

Children's imaginations are unreserved. A pencil is a magic wand, a cardboard tube a gilded trumpet; an ordinary room transforms into a fairy castle. To approach the act of writing as a child is to awaken the imagination to unexpected possibilities.

BY LIVING MINDFULLY, we can begin afresh with every period of meditation, every writing session. Again and again we find a space in which creativity can happen. This gives us a chance to view every experience without judgement or analysis, just as a child would.

Babies have no choice but to be open-minded to begin with, because they are born knowing nothing, and have to accept everything they see and hear. Not yet having learned discernment, the world is full of wonder for them.

Do you remember your childhood games? My friends and I longed to ride, and our imaginative play involved magical horses. We rode them through both earthly and heavenly landscapes because, conveniently, they could fly as well as run! A low wall between my parents' back garden and our neighbours' was our 'horse'. We were by turns cowgirls, Native Americans, racing jockeys and show jumpers. From our concrete mount we looked out over wide, wild vistas, heard the drumming of a thousand hooves on the prairie, or acknowledged the applause of enthusiastic crowds.

MINDFULNESS EXERCISE

A DAY OF 'WATCHING THE MIND'

For a day, as you go about your normal activities, give greater attention than usual to your mind and its processes. Are you irritated at slow traffic on the daily commute? Perhaps you meet a friend and feel a rush of gladness. You turn away from your work for a moment, feeling regretful that you are not free to ski, swim, write or sleep. Watch all of these emotions without judgement or analysis. When you can, make some written notes. How did the emotion feel? What triggered it and how did you experience any physical reactions to it? How could you use this emotion in your writing? Describe a fictional character affected by one of these emotions. What causes it? How does he react? Remember that his experience is not the same as yours. He is not you; he is your creation.

Our playtime was influenced by the world about us, our school lessons and the heroes we watched on TV or read about in books and comics. But our imaginations were certainly not limited to these. We invented, and became, our own heroes, giving ourselves tasks to accomplish, victims to save from danger and magical powers.

What If?

I like the idea of every writer having a sign pasted above their workplace with the words 'What if?' written in large type. It would help us remember to keep that child-like spirit of enquiry and inventiveness in our writing. Describing a character going about an everyday task, we can stop and ask: 'What if … there was an earthquake; a knock on the door; a power cut; an unexpected message?'

Children are endlessly inventive, trying things out just to see what will happen. My cousin's son got together with a friend and (with some adult supervision) welded pieces of

FROM MUNDANE TO EXTRAORDINARY

Children use everyday articles as objects of invention, and we can do the same. But everyday articles really do have potential beyond their normal uses.

The paperclip

In addition to its normal purpose of keeping several pages together, I have used a paperclip as: a plant tie, a picture hook, a stylus (to write in clay), a zip-pull, a temporary replacement for a missing button and a bookmark.

The brick

Even the most mundane article can be imbued with mystery and significance. Imagine a brick being used as: a weapon, a carrier for a message, a step up to a new life, a means of escape or a cover for a secret.

Think of another mundane object and make it extraordinary by imagining it being used to bring interest and drama into a scene you are writing.

metal into something they could use as a small cooker. They didn't follow instructions. They just tried it out, and it worked.

It's the same with mindfulness; it's the same with life; it's the same with writing. We only need an adventurous and inventive approach. It may not always result in success, but the whole point of invention is to find out what will happen when we try. Through failures and successes we learn, and so develop our skills. We only need the willingness to ask 'What if?'.

MINDFULNESS EXERCISE

REMEMBERING MINDFULLY

- Take your mind back to your childhood, to the times of friendship and play. Now choose writing materials that 'chime' with those times – perhaps using coloured inks and a bright notebook. Bring them to a quiet writing place and make yourself comfortable.
- In the spirit of child-like innocence, turn your attention to your breath. Even though you may already have called to mind some happy childhood memories, let them rest while you 'wait to write'. After some minutes of settling the mind with your perfectly innocent in-breaths and out-breaths, take up your writing materials and record some of the people, games and imaginative play of your childhood. What were your motivations for play? Where did you go in your mind, either alone or with your friends?
- If you like, expand on these recollections now, extending them in your imagination beyond those childhood games, yet all the while retaining the essence of child-like playfulness.

THE RAINBOW

To achieve a body of rainbow light is thought to be the ultimate attainment of the Buddhist practitioner – the highest state of enlightenment. For the ordinary writer, the rainbow can be seen as a great inspiration, heightening our creativity and filling our work with colour.

EVERYONE LOVES A RAINBOW, and most children know the sequence of rainbow colour in the spectrum of light: red, orange, yellow, green, blue, indigo, violet. What do these different colours mean to you? Do you have a favourite?

Blue

Although it is not the 'first' colour of the rainbow, I begin with blue, because blue is the colour of our sky, which makes our planet unique in the solar system, and is a wonder and delight to human beings. What does blue mean to you? When I was at junior school, my friend Sue was chosen to play Mary in the school nativity play. She wore a blue cloak for the part. I so wanted to be Mary and wear the blue cloak, but I had to be satisfied with being an angel, watching over the scene.

Green

I choose green next for the beauty and marvel of growing things. Green is the colour of growth, of life, of hope. For me, it's the colour of the English countryside in early summer, when every leaf is perfect and every plant reaching up to its fulfilment. Green is for the rainforests, lungs of the Earth, and green is the sea on a cloudy day. My study is painted a bright, lime green. It is always cheerful and uplifting. What does green mean to you?

Yellow

Yellow is for the sunshine, the source of all life on Earth. It is a light reflected in many beautiful, bright flowers. I remember driving through France one summer, with fields of yellow sunflowers as far as the eye could see, all of them turning to face the sun on its trajectory from dawn to dusk. A more personal memory of yellow is of my very first grown-up dress, an A-line style with long sleeves and a yellow paisley pattern. How I loved it. What are your thoughts on and memories of yellow? Do you love it too?

Indigo

Indigo is the colour of the sky at the furthest point of evening, before it tips into night. It's the deepest blue possible, seeming to hold the whole of the previous day in suspension, while it supports the stars as they begin to appear. To me, it seems the most profoundly spiritual of all the rainbow colours, most beautiful and mysterious. Although it is one of our most popular colours for dyeing cloth, I think indigo really belongs to the sky. Attempts to reproduce it can only fall short of that perfect final light of day. My memories of true indigo are of summer skies, studded with stars, clouded by the Milky Way. Untouchable, unreachable; the colour of dreams. What does indigo mean to you? A favourite pair of jeans? An evening walk in forest or desert?

Orange

Orange is the most cheerful of the colours. Fruits, flowers, the brilliant plumage of exotic birds, the flashing heart of an opal, the centre of a flame; all carry this warming, uplifting colour. Does orange have a place in your life? What memories does it bring? Orange reminds me of a crateful of the beautiful round fruit to which it gives its name, piled into a festive pyramid on a friend's sideboard. Orange is also the colour of an old rose in our garden. It was there when we moved in over twenty years ago, and still graces our lives with bright blooms every year from spring until winter.

Violet

Violet is a magisterial colour, a dye most precious and rare until recent years. It has associations of spirituality, wisdom and beauty. Coming at the 'end' of the usual list of rainbow colours and, indeed, at the end of the visible spectrum of light, it is yet highly valued. Violet is the colour of the amethyst ring on my finger as I write this. Violet gives its colour and its name to a small spring flower that grows wild in the British countryside and reminds me of walking in woodland with my mother. What is violet to you?

Red

Red is the first of colours, the famous celebrity that everybody loves. Red is the colour that any child will turn to and reach for with a smile. Red has a big personality: it shouts from warning signs and flags; announces approaching festivals, decorates lips and fingernails, gives importance to everything it touches. Red gets you noticed. And red is the colour of our own lifeblood. We carry it in our bodies, oxygenate it with every breath; red is part of being human. From schooldays, I remember red as a critical mark that my teacher inked in the margin of my schoolbook. And red is the colour of my favourite pair of boots. Polished, cared for and repaired

MINDFULNESS EXERCISE

PAINTING WITH THE IMAGINATION

Do you have a favourite colour? Write a piece about something with that colour. This could be a green field, a red car – anything you wish. Then, change the colour to something unlikely: the field becomes black; the car is streaked with gold. Why? Who is there? What has happened?

many times, they are old friends that always cheer me. What are your feelings and memories about this key colour? How has red affected your life?

Colour Vibration

Colour inspires our writing in many ways but, approached in a spirit of adventure, it can also influence our creativity at a deeper, vibrational level, closer to meditation than to memory. Unlike the previous suggestions, this is not intended necessarily to prompt written thoughts on a colour itself, coloured objects or colourful scenery. It is to let a colour sit in the mind before writing, allowing its vibrations to permeate our creativity.

RHYTHM IN MIND

Music is mysterious and almost magical. It seems to exemplify the Buddhist concept of impermanence; we cannot cling to it any more than we can hold the water of a flowing river. Perhaps because of its linear quality, music can inspire our writing and affect our mood as we write.

AS A TEENAGER, when I was studying for my school exams, it was easier for me to concentrate with the radio beside me, playing my favourite music. My parents couldn't understand it, but it worked for me, and for most of my

MINDFULNESS EXERCISE

A COLOUR WRITING-MEDITATION

- First, you need to find some coloured paper or card. Ideally, it's best to have one each of the rainbow colours: red, orange, yellow, green, blue, indigo and violet, with others in any in-between colours if you wish, but each sheet to be a single plain colour. Each piece of paper or card needs to be at least A4 size. This is so that it can fill the main part of your vision as you look at it.
- When you have collected the colours, prepare for a meditation and have your writing materials with you. Sit comfortably, noticing your in- and out-breaths and settling the mind. Remember that thoughts are to be acknowledged but the attention returned to the breath during this waiting period.
- When your mind feels settled, turn your attention to your collection of coloured papers. Choosing mindfully and intuitively, select one colour to begin with.
- Hold the coloured card a few inches from your face. There is no need to focus with your eyes or your thoughts, just relax and fill your awareness with the colour. Don't try to think of objects or memories associated with the colour, just absorb and enjoy it for its own sake.
- After a few minutes, move the card away and take a few mindful breaths, giving your eyes time to adjust. Then, begin to write your journal or whatever writing project you are currently engaged in.

The time spent with colour can bring about some powerful imaginative responses, and you may wish to try a colour-meditation with a different colour on another occasion.

friends too. That music played the rhythm of our developing lives and we responded with gratitude. Although my tastes changed as I got older, music continued to both inspire and calm me through the ups and downs of studying and writing. Most of us can be helped to feel relaxed by listening to gentle music, or be enlivened by an energetic tune. But music can also be strongly inspiring – stimulating memory and emotion. There is little more evocative than a tune, taking us back many years and creating in our bodies the same emotions that were caused by circumstances long gone. No wonder music inspires stories and poems.

A certain song reminds me of a time when I was standing in a hall among hundreds of people, and everyone spontaneously began to sing together. It was a very moving and almost electrifying experience in which I felt completely absorbed. If I want to write a scene of strong camaraderie between friends, I can play that song and, because I know it will revive that feeling, it helps me to express the same emotion through my fictional characters. When I use music for such a purpose, I don't actually write while it is playing but engage with the music mindfully, allowing myself to feel the emotions it brings without judgement, only later putting it into words.

Is there a piece of music or a song that has particular meaning to you? Just stop for a moment and call it to mind, noticing the emotions it provokes. Could you write how that feels, and perhaps confer a similar emotion on a fictional character?

The Mozart Effect

A study was once conducted where students were asked to undertake certain written tests while music of various types was being played. It was found that the students performed better to Mozart's music than any other. These findings have now been disputed, but we tried this in a class of students, just for fun, using Mozart as well as other types of music. Some students thought they wrote more creatively while the music was playing. Others didn't like the experience at all and found it difficult to concentrate. If you would like to try it, I suggest you choose a mixture of music, of various rhythms, because some might suit you better than others. This is to be played while you are actually writing, so it would probably be best for the music to be instrumental only, as words can be distracting, and this exercise is supposed to work at a subliminal level rather than directly inspiring ideas.

Personally, I am most likely to use music in this way when I feel tired or listless. On these occasions, I like to play high-tempo music, especially Celtic drum music. I cannot help but feel lively in the face of such sparkling rhythmic action!

Walking – The Rhythm of Inspiration

Those of us who are able to walk have the rhythm of inspiration literally at our feet. Most of my best writing ideas have come to me either during a walk or immediately afterwards – usually while I am actually walking.

The reasons for the inspirational benefits of walking may actually be proved scientifically. Walking makes our lungs work a little harder, flooding our blood with life-giving oxygen, which, in turn, revives our brain cells and helps us to think more creatively. Also, exercise infuses us with endorphins – the happiness hormones. This gives us a sense of wellbeing, which can help us to approach our creative ideas more positively.

I have heard that the associated benefits described above are true. But, for me, there's no need for scientific proof; I'm already convinced that the rhythm of walking is beneficial to my writing life. It's happened too many times for this to be coincidental.

> The great gift of walking is that it gives us time to think, letting thoughts and ideas develop at their own speed, at a natural bodily pace. Whether the walk is short or long, it gives us an uninterrupted opportunity to tease things out, getting a new perspective on a problem. We can reflect on our experiences, good or bad, get them into proportion, cast them into the form of a story; see the funny side.
>
> FROM 'THE ART OF MINDFUL WALKING'
> BY ADAM FORD

MINDFULNESS EXERCISE

A 'WALKING FOR WRITING' EXERCISE

In Chapter 2, I suggested a walking meditation for experiencing the elements. This time, I would like us to experience the rhythm of walking for its own sake, noticing mindfully how the action of walking might inspire ideas and solve writing problems.

- Take some writing materials with you on this walk. Just a pencil and pocket-sized notebook should be enough, in case you have ideas that need to be written down, so that you don't forget by the time you have arrived back home!
- Set off on a fairly familiar route, so that you don't need to give too much attention to direction or similar preoccupations. Just walk at an easy, rhythmic pace. At first, try to concentrate on the sensation of your feet moving over the ground. Notice how your body feels at the beginning of the walk and later as you have warmed into your pace. Allow thoughts and ideas to pass through your mind, watching and releasing them as you would in a meditation, but being mindful of anything inspirational that you can use for your writing.

Of course, brilliant and useful ideas will not always come to mind while walking. If by the time you reach home, nothing has occurred to you for your writing, then you will at least have had a beneficial walk in the open air. This should have energized and relaxed your body, a wonderful state in which to begin writing.

CHAPTER SIX

Being a Mindful Writer

The mindful writer sits at her desk. Within reach are the materials of her craft; in her head, the bright elements of imagination and inspiration. She is practised, she knows her own voice and her own mind. She is waiting to begin; for the nature of writing is to begin again and again. Mindfulness helps us begin with hope. It shows us the writer's pathway and guides us to enjoy every step. In this last chapter, we will be seeing with awareness the kind of writers we are, and by setting joyful intentions, we will be beginning again on that pathway.

Choosing to Write

Deciding to give time to our writing can be a courageous resolution. While our lives may be full of activity, with work, family and the daily tasks of normal life, we still wish to spend time exercising our creativity through writing. Choosing to do this requires mindful intention.

'What do you do?' This is quite a common question to come up in social situations when strangers are getting to know one another. The answer usually involves our working occupation. Pensioners might say 'I'm retired'. Parents could describe a busy life with children. Students might explain a challenging study course. Few of us would say 'I'm a writer', unless writing happens to be our main paid occupation. That's fine.

But if we turn inward and ask that same question of ourselves – 'What do you do?', how would we answer? Our lives are, of course, full of things we 'do', but some of us long to spend more time writing. We have worlds to create, stories to tell, feelings to express, beliefs to share, important, magical, ingenious things to say. Yet sometimes we almost think that we don't have the right to spend our time writing. Is it self-indulgent? Would we be better occupied with other activities?

No one except ourselves can answer that question. But if we decide that, yes, we want to be writers, we might need a plan. And, as with everything, our best and most hopeful plans begin with mindfulness.

Change

Impermanence is one of the three Seals of the Dharma – the Buddhist teachings. Although we often wish things to remain the same, they never can. Life, and we ourselves, are always in a condition of change. In whatever way we might try to predict the pattern of this change, it pulses and sparks with a life of its own that can bring sadness and joy beyond expectation. Change creates an adventure in the everyday. To embrace the reality of such uncertainty is to retain a peaceful mind within a dynamic existence.

Arguably, writers might understand this better than some, because the nature of writing is change. Like a river flowing, a story or poem moves from beginning to end. Change is an essential part of writing. And change happens when we make a clear decision that writing will be an important part of our lives.

This is no insignificant matter. Our habits, responsibilities and the opinions of others can give the appearance of putting obstacles in our path. Mindfulness will remind us that such obstacles are indeed just that – appearances to mind.

Are you willing to make a commitment to writing, giving it time and space in your life? If so, as with any other important change, it would be beneficial to have certain positive states of mind to begin with. And you can turn to your mindfulness practice to help you. If you would like to make this change with hope, you might find it helpful to try the exercise on the following page.

MINDFULNESS EXERCISE

A WRITER'S MEDITATION FOR CHANGE

- Take your writing materials to a space where you can be alone. Sit comfortably and begin to settle your mind, noticing your thoughts and allowing them to pass.
- Your mind is like a room full of busy thoughts, concerns and worries. But it's time to let them pass, to clear the space in order to receive something new in your life – a commitment to your writing. What positive qualities will you need for this to be successful? You may wish for energy, optimism, awareness; anything that seems right for you.
- Now, open your notebook and write the name of one of these qualities. Underneath, describe a memory of when you were in that state of mind. For example, if I write 'Energy' at the top of my page and wish to invoke this feeling, I might begin by remembering the sight of a recent new moon in a golden sky; or a song that lifted my mood years ago when I was looking for direction; or a retreat I attended recently that refreshed my creativity. Write in detail and, in particular, try to describe as closely as possible how you felt.
- Now, put your writing aside and concentrate on that feeling. Familiarize yourself with the feeling itself. Begin to detach it from the occasion or situation that originated it. Try to see the quality as a pure light that will infuse the 'room' of your mind, making it ready for this joyful change in your life ahead.

This is also a beautiful exercise to use in times of difficulty, perhaps if you are experiencing 'writer's block' or fear of criticism, or at any time you feel the need to 'begin again' positively with your writing.

Imagining the Writer

As writers, we can expect to have a good deal of imagination. This is invaluable for our writing, but it is also a useful attribute when making lifestyle changes. By imagining mindfully, we will make the changes that are right for us and become the writers we are meant to be.

It's true, of course, that to be writers, we need to write. But, as I mentioned previously, we often need to persuade ourselves that writing is an activity that is important to us.

I used to imagine that I would be a successful writer some day, but I actually saw myself in rather vague terms, having a great reputation (and earning a very large income!) even before I had any idea what I wanted to write. When meditation came into my life, *doing* the writing became more important than *being* a writer. However, I continued to imagine my life as a successful writer. Some of the images were very strong and, by looking mindfully at them, I was able to understand more clearly my own talents and preferences. One of the images was of travelling and talking to people in order to research my stories. Another involved running interesting workshops at literary events. By considering these images mindfully, I knew that, for me, they would be enjoyable aspects of the writing life, should I be given the opportunity.

MINDFULNESS EXERCISE

A 'WRITING THE WRITER' EXERCISE

Begin as usual, sitting upright but comfortable, concentrating on your breath, until your mind has begun to settle and a feeling of clarity emerges.

- Now, try to imagine the life of a successful writer. Don't dwell on her background, just be assured that this person is a lot like you – with similar commitments and responsibilities – but remember she is a successful writer.
- Make some notes on the following:

How mindful is this writer?
Does she create clarity and space in the mind while 'waiting to write'?
Where do you see this writer working?
What sort of room is she in?
Is she at a desk or table?
Is there a pen or pencil in her hand?
Is she using a laptop or tablet?
When and for how much time is she in her writing space? Say, four-hourly periods without a break – or twenty-minute flurries with lots of tea breaks?

What kind of people does she know?
How does she contact and interact with them?
Who are her favourite authors and what does she like to read?
Can you imagine the style and colours of the clothes she wears?
What does this person write (poetry, blogs, stories, letters, novels, biography, film scripts, or a mixture)?
How does this successful writer respond to criticism of her work?
How does she respond to rejection of her work?
How does she respond to praise of her work?

When you have finished, take time to settle the mind again. Then review your notes. What positive changes could you make so that your life more closely resembles that of your 'successful writer'? If some of the changes seem too daunting, they might not be for you. Others could be simply fun and delightful, as I discovered for myself.

The 'Writing the Writer' exercise on the previous two pages is quite a fun way of mindfully addressing our own expectations and preferences with regard to the writing life. Suitably, it also exercises the imagination.

The Tasselled Scarf

One of the questions in that exercise reminds me of an occasion when I realized that by making some small, seemingly insignificant changes, I could begin to feel differently about my life and look on myself as a writer.

I overheard two people talking about a writer I knew and admired called Debbie. One of them said, 'What do you think about the way she dresses?'

'Well,' answered the other, 'her clothes are unconventional, but she's one of those artistic types – a writer, I think. I suppose she just dresses to reflect her personality.'

As I listened to them, I thought, 'But Debbie's clothes are great. I'd love to dress like that.' This might seem trivial, but overhearing that conversation seemed very significant to me. Later, I decided to give it some mindful attention. I took some quiet time alone. Breathing steadily, I began to settle my mind. After a while, I called that overheard conversation to mind. In the clarity that comes with a settled mind, I understood that I'd been walking around as someone who admired writers, loved reading, enjoyed writing, but had no real belief that the writing life was for me. Thinking of Debbie, I knew she was

someone who saw herself – and expected others to see her – as a writer. Because of that, because she felt and looked like a writer, she encouraged herself to be the very best writer she could be. At least, that's what I thought.

The Writer in the Mirror

Of course, this isn't really about clothes at all, but about self-awareness, about noticing our own actions, about giving time to what is important to us. It helped me to see that, despite the duties and responsibilities of my life, there was a real yearning in me to tell stories, to present them in the most engaging way I could, and to do my best – whatever level of talent or ability I possessed. I wanted to look in the mirror each morning and see a writer.

Fortunately, of course, this didn't mean buying a whole new wardrobe of 'writer' clothes. But, from that day, I began to walk around as a writer. Nobody knew, of course, but I knew, and it made a difference to me. I began to give myself writing time, to see this as at least equally important as other duties and responsibilities. I watched less television, spent less time on the internet, did less housework. I spent the extra time writing; I was becoming a writer.

Not long afterwards, I bought myself a new scarf with coloured tassels. I loved it. But please don't imagine that I think a tasselled scarf will turn anyone into a writer. I know plenty of writers who would never want to dress as I do. Even

so, they dress as the writers they are; they look in the mirror in the morning and see a writer. They endeavour to be the best writers they can be.

Keeping a Positive Mind

What is a writer's life like? There must be a different answer to this question for every writer who exists. But, like any other work, writing can bring both problems and satisfaction. In order to avoid despondency, we need to keep a positive mind with regard to our work.

You will have gathered by now that I believe mindfulness is essential to my writing life. If I get out of the habit of regular meditation, if I forget to settle and clear my mind while 'waiting to write', then my writing – and my life – suffers.

The writer's life can be full of enjoyment, fulfilment, energy, friendship, support and delight. It can also bring problems, rejection, disappointment, loneliness, criticism and tight deadlines. However, and most importantly, the mindful writer understands that all the positive and negative aspects of the writer's life, all the failures and successes, are simply appearances to mind. The mindful writer can settle, clear and control the mind, aware of thoughts that are helpful or unhelpful to the purpose of our writing. This sounds wonderful – but it's not always so easy.

Writer's Block

'Writer's block' is a condition in which a writer feels unable to progress with a writing project, or in fact finds they cannot produce any new work at all. They sense a loss of creativity and their writing seems banal and uninteresting; to continue seems pointless.

One of the main reasons for writer's block is fear. I may have enjoyed writing my book, but as the project nears completion and it's almost time for others to read it, I suddenly lose all confidence. One way through this fear for me is to breathe calmly, smile and remember that, of all the people in the world, I am the one who cares most about my own project. No one else will lose sleep over it, so why should I? This attitude can help to reduce my self-importance and allow me to continue steadily with my work.

Another 'block' is often that we can't stop editing our work, trying to perfect every sentence, so we never progress beyond the first few chapters. In this case, it's best to scribble away, ignoring possible imperfections, and leave the editing until the end. In fact, for me this is a treat I look forward to, as I thoroughly enjoy editing my own work, although I know this isn't true for all writers. Whether or not you enjoy editing, it's better to feel 'stuck' with a completed manuscript in your hands rather than just one chapter.

When feeling completely 'blocked', remember your mindfulness practice. After some minutes of noticing your

breathing, perhaps invoking 'Peace' for the in-breath and 'Calm' for the out-breath, take your pen in your hand and write about your feelings. What do you think has caused the block? Write down the aspects you like and dislike about your writing. If appropriate, have a 'conversation' with some of the characters, as suggested in Chapter 4 (see pages 96–9). It's better to write something, rather than nothing, and this in itself can 'unstick' the block.

The Deadline – The Lifeline

Of the writers I know, most of them love to have a publisher's deadline, a date on which the work must be finished. This, surely, is no 'deadline' but really a 'lifeline'. It's the point at which our work lives – the point of birth, really, where what is written becomes what is read. I think one of the main reasons a piece of work doesn't get completed is that no one is waiting for it. This is where our sangha companions can help us. I once had an agreement with a friend that we would get together in three months' time with a completed novel. Because I knew she was expecting me to do it and waiting to read it, I did manage to complete the manuscript, and this was a great help to me. So, if you are not in the extremely helpful situation of having a publisher's commitment, with its attendant 'deadline' to concentrate your mind and provide a true 'lifeline' for your work, why not ask one of your writing sangha friends to help instead?

The Critic

For a writer, criticism can be hard to take. Our writing sometimes seems like a newborn baby to us: it might not look perfect to others, but we love it, and have the instinct to protect it with our lives. So criticism of our new creation is never welcome. However, receiving criticism gets easier with experience and can even be looked on positively.

When I receive criticism of my writing, it can hurt. So I have learned to leave it aside for a while (a couple of days if possible), and later bring it to a quiet session of mindfulness meditation. At that point, I will know if the criticism is valid or not. If not, I put it from my mind and proceed with my work. If I find the criticism is valid, then I try to see it as a great opportunity for improving my work. After all, why wouldn't I want to improve? When this happens, I know criticism is a good thing, allowing positive development – even though it sometimes causes growing pains.

It is also worth remembering that the person offering the criticism will, more than likely, feel uncomfortable about having to tell us that our work needs improving. So let's try to treat them, and ourselves, with mindful compassion. If we react with aggression, they will feel attacked and will be unlikely to want to help us again. Mindfulness can improve all our relationships, and is the perfect way of accepting and calming our emotions, so that we will not stumble over them on our way to becoming better writers.

Laugh!

The Laughing Buddha was a monk who chuckled at life no matter whether his experiences were difficult, beautiful or painful. We can't be expected always to laugh with the wisdom of the Buddha, but we can try to take ourselves and our concerns less seriously, and laugh more often, whether our problems come from writer's block, deadlines, criticism or simple fear. Laughter has a real effect on the brain, making us feel brighter, dispelling anxiety and actually improving our problem-solving ability and creativity.

Laughter has a real effect on the brain

Try a laughing meditation now. You don't need to think of something funny; just take one or two mindful breaths to relax and clear the mind. Then smile – just a small one to begin with. Smile to the Buddha; smile to your own precious life. Now, extend it to a big smile and chuckle a little. If you can, make it a full-bodied laugh. Relax and then try again. How do you feel? I just tried it and the experience left my whole body feeling fresher. It may seem silly to laugh at nothing, but no one needs a reason to feel good.

The Laughing Buddha reminds us to be light-hearted with regard to our writing. Mindfulness helps us reflect this attitude in our lives, enhancing our creativity, awareness and compassion, so that our writing will be the very best it can be, bringing joy to ourselves and others.

JOY

My name is Joy. And, from an early age, I've known it's a word that isn't just about me. It has a clear meaning in English that I think is on the 'lighter and brighter' side of happiness. When people hear my name, they sometimes make jokes – especially when I'm obviously not having a good day. Joy is a name to live up to, perhaps. I was never very comfortable with it until mindfulness and writing came together in my life. Since then, I have been glad to attach my name to one of the most joyful activities of my life.

When I began to meditate, I was guided and inspired by that little book with the torn cover by Osho. From him, I understood that meditation is delightful for its own sake – not to achieve, to combat, to win, to survive – but for the simple joy of meditation. I am convinced of this truth. It makes me smile. And yet, I believe that mindfulness meditation can bring this simple joy into any of the activities we choose to do and, for me, especially into my writing. With mindfulness, there's a joyful quality in practice, research, editing, in the self-awareness that feeds the imagination. Mindfulness guides me into writing in the style and on the subjects that are right for me, and brings joy into my connection with my writing sangha friends. Because of mindfulness, we can write for the simple joy of writing itself.

And as I sit by the window of my favourite café with the sun on my shoulders, writing these final lines of this book, I sincerely wish for you what I have myself in these moments: I wish you joy in your writing.

FURTHER READING & INSPIRATION

In addition to those authors referred to or quoted in the book, here are just a few of the novelists and poets who inspire me:
Maya Angelou
Simon Armitage
Philippa Gregory
Seamus Heaney
Jackie Kay
Hilary Mantel
Ruth L. Ozeki
Terry Pratchett
J. K. Rowling
Carol Shields
Salley Vickers

Over the years, many books have helped and motivated me with my writing and my mindfulness practice. Some are already mentioned in this book. Others are given below.

For Writing

Julia Bell & Paul Magrs (eds) *The Creative Writing Coursebook*, Macmillan, 2001.

Julia Cameron *The Artist's Way*, Pan Boo (Macmillan), 1995.

Janet Sternburg (ed.) *The Writer on Her Work*, Virago Press, 1992.

Christopher Vogler *The Writer's Journey*, Michael Wiese Productions, 2007.

There are plenty of websites for writers. Here are two that are particularly helpful:

www.youwriteon.com
Provides the opportunity for writers to engage with each others' work, and there's a chance for high-rated authors to receive advice from top publishers.

www.nownovel.com
Includes a blog by writer Bridget McNulty, which many writers find helpful. The posts are short and easy to follow.

For Mindfulness & Spirituality

Pema Chodron *Practicing Peace in Times of War*, Shambhala Publications, Inc., 2007.

Michael Dawson *The Findhorn Book of Forgiveness*, Findhorn Press, 2003.

Adam Ford *The Art of Mindful Walking*, Leaping Hare Press, 2012.

Geoffrey Durham *Being a Quaker – A Guide for Newcomers*, Quaker Quest, 2011.

Ruth Lauer-Manenti *An Offering of Leaves*, Lantern Books, 2009.

Thich Nhat Hanh *Cultivating the Mind of Love*, Parallax Press, 2008.

Thich Nhat Hanh *How to Walk*, Parallax Press, 2014.

Sister Dang Nghiem *Mindfulness as Medicine*, Parallax Press, 2015.

INDEX

The Mindfulness Series

The Art of Mindful Baking
Julia Ponsonby

The Art of Mindful Birdwatching
Claire Thompson

The Art of Mindful Gardening
Ark Redwood

The Art of Mindful Silence
Adam Ford

The Art of Mindful Singing
Jeremy Dion

The Art of Mindful Walking
Adam Ford

Einstein & the Art of Mindful Cycling
Ben Irvine

Galileo & the Art of Ageing Mindfully
Adam Ford

Happiness and How it Happens
The Happy Buddha

The Heart of Mindful Relationships
Maria Arpa

The Mindful Art of Wild Swimming
Tessa Wardley

Mindful Thoughts for Cyclists
Nick Moore

Mindful Thoughts for Walkers
Adam Ford

Mindfulness & Compassion
The Happy Buddha

Mindfulness and Surfing
Sam Bleakley

Mindfulness & the Art of Drawing
Wendy Ann Greenhalgh

Mindfulness & the Art of Managing Anger
Mike Fisher

Mindfulness & the Art of Urban Living
Adam Ford

Mindfulness & the Journey of Bereavement
Peter Bridgewater

Mindfulness & the Natural World
Claire Thompson

Mindfulness at Work
Maria Arpa

Mindfulness for Black Dogs & Blue Days
Richard Gilpin

Mindfulness for Unravelling Anxiety
Richard Gilpin

The Mindfulness in Knitting
Rachael Matthews

Moments of Mindfulness

Naturally Mindful

Zen & the Path of Mindful Parenting
Clea Danaan

Acknowledgements

First, I want to thank the wonderful Dharma teachers – especially Geshe Kelsang Gyatso and Thich Nhat Hanh – who brought mindfulness to the West, and my own meditation teacher Kelsang Rak-Ma from the Amitabha Centre in Bristol, for her kind and accessible teaching, and her laughter. Thank you to the delightful Leaping Hare team, particularly Monica Perdoni, Jenni Davis, Stephanie Evans and Fleur Jones, for giving me the opportunity of writing this book and for their help and enthusiasm. I want to extend my gratitude to Paul Fletcher of the Chalice Well in Glastonbury for his help and inspiration and for allowing me to include the quote from his book on page 78. Thank you to the members of my meditation and writing sanghas, especially to June's group, Syreeta and George, Woodspring Word Weavers, Weston Poets, Annie Merrin and Karen Gunning. Finally, my heartfelt thanks to my husband Bob for his constant and generous support, and for all the cups of Joy tea.

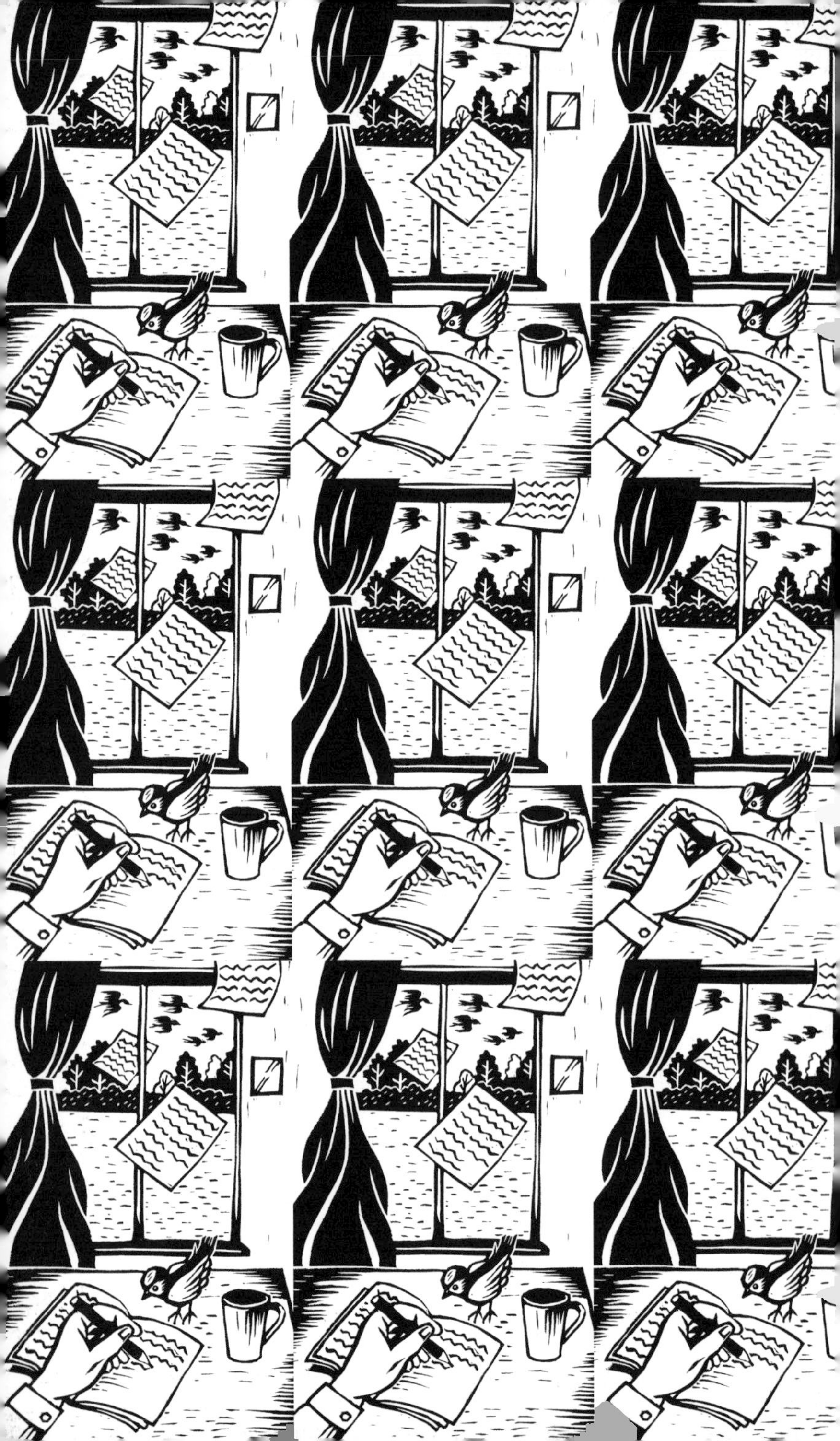